The Fiesta Culture

How America "Celebrates" Hispanic Culture and Trivializes Hispanic People

By

D. Russell Martinez

ISBN: 978-1-4033-1532-8 (sc)
ISBN: 978-1-4033-1533-5 (hc)
ISBN: 978-1-4033-1531-1 (e)

Library of Congress Control Number: 2002103936

Print information available on the last page.

This book is printed on acid-free paper.

1stBooks - rev. 05/28/21

Dedicated to my mother, Sophie Martinez, without whose encouragement and support this book could not have been written. Her belief in the ideas of the book was a continuing inspiration, just as her life itself has been an inspiration for all who have taken heart from her courage and strength in the face of hardship and adversity.

TABLE OF CONTENTS

CHAPTER 1

THE FIESTA CULTURE

"Every life needs a little Salsa"
—"Chi Chi's" Mexican Restaurants' slogan

"Life always needs a little Salsa"
—"Chi Chi's" Mexican Restaurants' *revised* slogan

The "salsafication" (rhymes with falsification) of America is fully underway, enabling Americans everywhere to enjoy—if not a spicier, more interesting life—tortilla chips topped with melted *nacho* cheese and jalapeno slices or *picante* sauce.

The point at which this "salsafication" hit its full stride—or became *fully strident* at least in American popular culture—may be dated to the early 1990's, not because it verged upon the 500th Anniversary of Columbus' "discovery" of the New World, but because it marked the first time ever that sales of salsa *picante* sauce surpassed ketchup in the United States.

At the time, record-breaking, ketchup kickin' salsa was hailed in the popular media as a symbol of non-Hispanic Americans' "discovery" of authentic Hispanic culture. And ever since, salsa has been widely served up as a convenient, compelling metaphor for Hispanics and Hispanic culture.

This simplification of Hispanics—of who Hispanics *are*, and what they *offer* to *other* Americans—is a kind of salsafication as well, a pungent sharpening of perception itself.

And it all folds in very neatly with the contemporary celebration in pop culture of the *fiesta* as the vehicle to carry salsafication forth to the far-flung reaches of America (and the world), and of Hispanics and Hispanic culture as the source of "salsafied" fiesta spirit to enliven other Americans' lives.

The extraordinary story of how "salsafication" is infusing American popular culture and American life more generally—effecting the wholesale transfer, the *transfusion* of Hispanic spirit

1

from Hispanic people to non-Hispanics—and what this means for Hispanic-Americans and for our country is the story of this book.

And although *salsafication* is often portrayed and promoted as a tribute to Hispanic people and their culture, it is, in fact, *in effect*, nothing of the sort.

The success of "salsafication" is less about Hispanics—as will become all too clear—than it is about the primacy of pop culture's appeal to the senses and emotions. "Salsafied" Hispanic spirit is simply becoming a featured part, a bigger player, in this appeal to consumers in American popular culture.

Salsafication's real strength thus lies in the self-interest, in the apparent *longing*, of individual non-Hispanic Americans for what they see as enlivening Hispanic spirit.

The Scramble to "Salsafy"

Pop culture's creative people are scrambling as fast as they can to "salsafy" us, often following on, *falling over*, each other's "salsafication" metaphors.

The competition to characterize Hispanic life and culture as a source of enlivening spirit for non-Hispanics, and then coordinate its efficient "downloading" into pop culture's "salsafied" products and entertainments, is more intense than ever. And the enthusiasm that pop culture's marketers and promoters bring to this task is palpable—and catching.

The excitement in pop culture over the perceived value and potential of "salsafied" Hispanic spirit—its ability to make money as it energizes the spirits of millions of non-Hispanic Americans (and millions more around the world)—seems to be boundless, bountiful enough to help sell all kinds of things that have nothing directly to do with Hispanics.

In whatever category of consumer one falls at any particular time, this can come home to one. Sometimes literally, as when one is a homeowner, for example—for those who are so situated—and what happens by turning on the television and seeing commercials for, say, "Fiesta Orange House Paint." Slap a coat of "Fiesta Orange" on the walls of your "recreation room" and you've suddenly imported the spirit of the *fiesta* into your daily life, into your *home!*

Bizarrely—but all too understandably, considering the effort that pop culture invests in "salsafication"—the spicy, passionate Hispanic world existing *somewhere*, from which the resonance to revitalize us (the non-Hispanic ones of "us") originates, takes on plausibility, a tangibility that seems perfectly comprehensible. When the logic is spun out from this source of "salsafication", all kinds of things become clear, and all sorts of problems get solved.

Hispanics are "contributing" to America, its morale and life, as never before, even if they are losing something *as individual people*. For salsafication is a group thing, and any considerations of Hispanics as complex, individual people aren't very helpful to its resonance for the white (and other non-Hispanic) Americans who want it.

Particular Hispanics—entertainers and actors, notably—may bring a new nuance, a fresh face or beguiling presence that helps to vary the *persona* of Hispanic spirit presented in pop culture and to keep it vital as it does its job of "salsafying" non-Hispanic spirits across America. But they are not changing its essential nature, and, with time, another new face, another Hispanic entertainer or actor will come along to exemplify Hispanic fiesta spirit.

And if Hispanics are contributing their very spirit, and white (and other non-Hispanic) Americans are eagerly seeking to engage some of this "salsafied" Hispanic spirit to enliven their own spirits, well, then, the problem of Hispanic "assimilation"—the obstacles to the addition of a Hispanic mosaic in the American model of "multiculturalism"— has been overcome.

If the logic of this pop culture-generated Hispanic model escapes some Hispanic-Americans—seeing as how, for example, it doesn't deal with or focus on the very real needs of Hispanic-Americans ranging from education and employment to political and economic empowerment—it is because Hispanic-Americans are themselves failing to "get with the program," as the saying goes.

Hispanics who can't—or won't—recognize that their enlivening spirit is helping to energize the new spirit of America, the *National Fiesta*, figuratively speaking, of America's exuberant affluence and hedonistic pursuit, are simply "party poopers." And nobody likes a person—or a people—who puts a damper on his or her party.

Of course, it is increasingly of little interest—for the purposes of any non-Hispanic American's "self-salsafication"—what Hispanics think. Hispanics, as people, are becoming ever more irrelevant to the process of drawing Hispanic spirit from Hispanic people to give to non-Hispanic people.

On a grandly absurd scale, Hispanic people are being replaced by the resonance of their "salsafied" spirit, even as they are "celebrated" in America.

Thus, the much-heralded Hispanic *Renaissance* (proclaimed in the media, by politicians, and by corporate leaders) is really a Hispanic *Resonance.*

Pop culture has already proven the pivotal point—Hispanic spirit is separable from Hispanic people, and can be used, as a Hispanic Extract (like vanilla extract) to flavor absolutely (it seems) anything, regardless of what Hispanics might think.

This is who Hispanics are, even if, on occasion, they don't understand it themselves. They are *salsafied*, and this *salsafied* spirit is too important, too potentially valuable to non-Hispanic Americans to be left to Hispanic people. Hispanics who don't want to share their spirit—in practical terms this is impossible, obviously—or don't like the idea of their spirit being "sublet" not only leave themselves open to the charge of being party poopers but stingy, too.

The scary part of this is how easily "salsafied" Hispanic resonance and elements are being carried far beyond the traditional boundaries of pop culture, a tribute to the charm and piquancy Hispanic elements hold to people who use them in other areas of American life, like politics and serious public policy issues in our ongoing "national dialogue."

Things like the decision over who should be the President of the United States and the facts we need to develop insightful views about international relations and important foreign leaders are among those being simplified, *salsafied*, to a startlingly simplistic level.

When the reporters and correspondents of one of the nation's leading newspapers begin to regularly use Hispanic elements to spice up, to *salsafy* their serious reportage, our national discourse is in free fall.

During the 2000 presidential campaign, *Washington Post* political reporter David Von Drehle wrote a Jan. 12, 2000 "Campaign Diary" dispatch entitled "Two Challengers Aim Beyond Male Bonding," analyzing the then leading candidates and their differing appeal to men and women. John McCain was more popular with men than his Republican rival George W. Bush, while on the Democratic side Bill Bradley won out with men over then-Vice President Al Gore.

The report pointed out how McCain had apparently earned this support by, among other things, enduring "years of sadistic torture" as a POW in North Vietnam during the Vietnam War.

"Bradley has his own *macho credentials {italics added}*, of course," the article went on, saying these credentials had been built from Bradley's years as a top college and professional athlete.

Any idea this was some sort of fluke at the prestigious *Post*—an example of the newspaper's editors having missed something—was put to rest when, a few months later, on May 8, 2000, the *Post* ran an article by Daniel Williams, one of its foreign correspondents, on the leader of Russia, Vladimir Putin. This report was aimed at informing readers about the personality of the new head of the Russian government and was headlined "Putin's Macho Style Leaves Some Wondering About Substance."

"Putin, who was inaugurated today…has introduced a *macho style* to the presidency…" the article detailed.

These articles were meant to be earnest efforts to help us understand the potential leaders of America and the new leader of Russia, using the *language* of *SalsaSpeak* and the echoes of Hispanic Resonance.

How all this has happened, how this incredible achievement—absurd as it is—has come to be so significant and singular an influence in American life, and what it means for *all* Americans, can best be understood by examining pop culture and the creation of *meaning*.

Realms of Meaning—The Popular-Culture-As-Vampire-Model

> "Human beings live in the realm of meanings. We do not experience pure circumstances; we always experience circumstances in their significance for men."
>
> —Alfred Adler, in **What Life Should Mean To You**, published in 1931

The act of drawing Hispanic spirit from Hispanic people to give to non-Hispanics—the idea that such a thing is not only possible but also plausible—may be one of the great triumphs of pop culture.

Creating this *meaning* of Hispanics and their special contributions to America—the magnitude of this achievement—is something that cannot be overstated. For this meaning is what drives and develops the applications of "salsafication," the myriad ways in which it works its way through pop culture and into American life more broadly.

And it is almost impossible—especially for anyone who has also been influenced by pop culture entertainments—to describe what is happening without using the metaphor of Pop-Culture-As-Vampire (or the idea of the nation's blood banks at work).

Pop culture's ability to figuratively spirit away the vital essences of Hispanics to give to non-Hispanics has—and the metaphorical connection to this aspect of the great vampire movies is truly inescapable—made Hispanic *people* less vital to our country even as their spirit becomes an ever-greater energizer of the nation's "life-blood."

This meaning of Hispanics for non-Hispanics—spurred by the self-interest of people who want to "salsafy" their non-Hispanic spirits from Hispanic spirits—is also quite able to overcome common sense and reality.

And it seems to start for pop culture, simply enough—for pop culture's Hispanic model of meaning—with the *fiesta*.

The Hispanic world opens to one, most richly reveals itself, with inviting, enticing images—if only in the "mind's eye"—of the *fiesta*.

Meaning, of course, is encoded in language and pop culture's creation of meaning about Hispanics is driven by its own little "language," *SalsaSpeak*.

SalsaSpeak is the use of Spanish-language and Hispanic elements to spice up American speech and perception. And the first and foremost part of SalsaSpeak is the word *fiesta*.

This is the setting in which one's sensory exploration of the spicy Hispanic world *of meaning* can be conducted—and pop culture's "tour guides" are eager to get you started, because there is a lot to "see" and "do."

Take, for example, the book "**Fiesta! A Celebration of Latin Hospitality**," by Anya Von Bremzen, published in 1997. On the book's "jacket," the reader is given a preview of what to expect inside, to wit, "In 'Fiesta,' Anya Von Bremzen perfectly captures the zest and exuberance of Latin food and traditions along with the joyous spirit of the Latin people."

And this "**Fiesta!**" book by Bremzen—born in Moscow, Russia but transplanted to the United States—is offered as a way to understand Hispanics *everywhere*.

The book jacket goes on to describe how "short essays, side notes, and the recipe introductions all evoke the vibrant music, zest for life, and festive traditions that light up not only the small towns and major cities of Latin America, Portugal, and Spain, but also the burgeoning Latino communities of the United States."

Not every non-Hispanic in the United States will have the time, money—or interest—to travel to all those places to commune with Hispanics and enjoy their fiestas, of course, but not to worry.

As the book jacket advises, "reading and looking through **Fiesta!** will make you want not only to cook these dishes for friends and family but also to turn up the music and dance to a seductive Latin beat."

That is about as self-contained in one's abode a world tour as possible—but it doesn't seem out of place in the practice of American popular culture.

The fiesta—its spirit and elements (of food and drink, music, dance and design, principally)—is an organizing principle here, not only for directing non-Hispanics' pursuit of Hispanic "salsafication" but also for helping non-Hispanic people "understand" Hispanics.

Reducing Hispanics to their sensory and emotional experiences—*salsafying* them in order for them to be able to *salsafy* us (the parts of *us* in America that are non-Hispanic)—and then treating this view as "knowledge" that can be easily extended in all kinds of ways shows how *meaning* about Hispanics is being created.

There is in all this (for pop culture and its consumers) a familiarity with Hispanic life and culture—a sense of *knowing* about Hispanic life and culture—and a seemingly effortless ability to apply this "knowledge" of the Hispanic world to non-Hispanic situations and things.

The long-standing stereotypes and "Storylines" of Hispanics as alternately happy and childlike Fiesta People or, to put it mildly, the kind of passionate Fiesta People whose celebrations inevitably get out of hand, have helped to prepare the way.

(Remarkably, the blatantly negative stereotypes and portrayals of Hispanics in the popular media still retain their powerful resonance in the midst of the current "celebration" of Hispanics, something that helps give the lie to the sincerity of that celebration of Hispanic peoples.)

But the familiarity has also been buoyed more recently by the powerful way in which pop culture can convey to people what is important at any given moment, what is "hot," as they say.

And Hispanics are "hot" right now, popular culture tells us, have been for some time, and are only getting hotter as time goes by.

This change in the "climate" of the country is being measured in American life by, among others, the national newsmagazines of Time and Newsweek, both of which had cover stories on Hispanics in 1999 to alert Americans to just how "hot" Hispanics were becoming, Moreover, Hispanics' "salsafied" or fiesta spirit seems to perfectly symbolize the larger idea of sharpening sensation—not limited to the effects of Hispanic elements—as the underlying principle of our emerging "Fiesta Culture" in America.

"Salsafied" Hispanic elements are being welcomed by American pop culture into a larger foundation of hedonism, in which one's own sensory experiences are elevated, *exalted*, as a validation of personal experience. That certainly seems to have occurred to pop culture's creative people—from movie scriptwriters and advertising copywriters to promoters of every kind of public event.

The fiesta, in fact, appears to be uniquely qualified to represent the hyper, heightened sense of fun that non-Hispanic Americans are after (and that pop culture is telling them they deserve).

Even when something has nothing directly to do with a Hispanic fiesta and its elements (of food and drink, music, dance, and design), the resonance of the fiesta spirit is sought out to offer a kind of validation, it seems, to the event or entertainment at hand.

Only the fiesta spirit seems able to soar with this new American spirit, like in, say—to pluck an example out of the air—the 1999 "International Hot Air Balloon Fiesta," held in New Mexico. (One might be tempted to explain this event away by noting how it took place in New Mexico, where many Hispanics live and which has a rich Hispanic history and heritage. This explanation, however, would not cover the 1999 companion "International Hot Air Balloon Fiesta" held in *Australia*.)

And it seems perfectly plausible when, playing off this resonance, other parts of pop culture and American life take this fiesta spirit as something actually existing, something tangible to be added to, something that is treated as fact and a form of *knowledge*.

A public television documentary on the balloon event in New Mexico was entitled "A Fiesta in the Sky." Someone with a literal mind—or an old-fashioned "linear" mind—might have wondered whether airborne mariachis were aloft with the other ballooners, and whether food caterers in another balloon went to each balloon in turn to provide healthy helpings of Mexican food.

But such a mindset is not millennium-ready, out of touch in the 21st Century in which we live.

The National "Fiesta"

As the "Balloon Fiesta" demonstrates, non-Hispanic promoters can straightforwardly, *straight facedly*, celebrate the "fiesta"—and the resonance of a spicy Hispanic world *somewhere* in which a full-blown fiesta is always going on and happy Hispanics are perpetually at play.

It's significant how non-Hispanics are able to be—are proving to be—the most influential exponents of the Hispanic fiesta, its spirit and elements, and its value to Americans.

Hispanics apparently have no proprietary control over their own spirit. Hispanics don't *own* their own spirit—or the Hispanic fiesta and its elements, which perfectly express and capture in tangible *objects* the fiesta spirit.

The ease with which non-Hispanics package and promote their "salsafied" products as "containing" (or resonating with) Hispanic spirit is a matter of reducing or "distilling" Hispanics to their sensory and emotional sensations.

Best of all, popular culture makes it easy to obtain such spirit without the intervening need for actual Hispanic human beings, offering proliferating numbers of "salsafied" Hispanic products in their stead (like salsa *picante* sauce and the tortilla chips that go with them) to fit practically any taste or desire.

"Chi Chi's" Mexican Restaurant chain—with its mottos and "Declaration of Salsafication"—shows how easily this is being accomplished.

No explicit reference to Hispanic people is needed, as long as the resonance of Hispanic spirit (with salsa becoming an all-purpose metaphor for happy Hispanic spirit) is a vital evocation. This enjoyment of Hispanic fiesta elements is enriched and enhanced by the richly evocative resonance of the "salsafied" Hispanic world where Hispanics are having the same sensory experiences. After all, non-Hispanics also have senses and emotions—taste buds and a capacity for excitement, for example—and thus all the requisite abilities to feel (when coupled with the right "salsafied" products to suit their tastes and interests) *like* a Hispanic.

The enjoyment by non-Hispanics of spicy Hispanic food, dance, music—and fiesta spirit—doesn't specifically exclude any presence of actual Hispanics.

But even if one wants to commune with the hedonistic Hispanics being "celebrated" by one's own engagements (with one's own sensory faculties) with the supposed sensory experiences of Hispanics, the quality and character of these connections are of a particularly suspect kind. One can satisfy this interest in having direct contact with hedonistic Hispanics—to see them *in action* as they enjoy the sensory satisfactions of fiesta elements and fiesta spirit—by being *around* Hispanics in a festive setting rather than *with* them as companions and friends.

For those who are less ambitious or less energetic, pop culture offers a way to enter the Hispanic world, to enjoy its hedonistic treasures, all without having to go anywhere or to be with real Hispanics. This Hispanic world works best as a "virtual" world that can be experienced from pop culture's "salsafied" products.

When completely successful—and that determination depends, of course, on the individual, varying, perhaps wildly, from person to person—the enjoyment of Hispanic elements resonating with Hispanic fiesta spirit is supposed to make one feel like a Hispanic, to make of one a "surrogate" Hispanic. At least temporarily, anyway, although the definite movement of our popular culture is to help instill in one a more or less permanent (if sometimes passively residing) fiesta spirit that can rise to the occasion. This is the import, for example, of living what has been called "A Fiesta Lifestyle" (as in one guidebook to San Antonio, Texas extolling such a lifestyle as one of the virtues of living, or simply visiting, this city).

As this Hispanic Resonance infuses popular culture and American life—like enrapturing ethers in some science fiction movie—there appears to be no area of our national life in which it does not come into play.

Hispanics are still available for blatantly negative portrayals as the kind of Fiesta People who can be expected to get out of hand. This means that even as some non-Hispanics are eagerly trying to become "surrogate" Hispanics—at least temporarily, when the mood strikes them—Hispanics can still serve as models of "bad" people not to be emulated in the "Storylines" of pop culture entertainments.

The fact that these compelling, contradictory views of Hispanics can co-exist for pop culture (and individual, non-Hispanic Americans) is quite remarkable, and represents Hispanic Resonance's ease and expansion in the handling of the malleable mental "materials" regarding the "salsafied" Hispanic world.

Pop culture is able to deftly exploit both these competing (albeit stereotypical) views in the service of "salsafication" for non-Hispanic Americans.

Take "macho," for example.

It began life—in its pop culture applications—as a view of domineering and violent Hispanic men. And although it is still available for such uses, it has come a long way since then.

11

In the already noted *Washington Post* articles on the possible future leaders of America (one of them now the current President) and the present leader of Russia, another kind of "macho" is presented.

This is the "good" macho, the *necessary* macho, the *leadership* macho. Leadership "macho" appears to be a newer twist in "macho" (in non-military applications of "macho," anyway), a newer variety of SalsaSpeak, which is supremely able to handle the wide (and wild) swings of meaning of Hispanic elements, from "good" to "bad" and back again, with potentially all the nuances in between.

Without a doubt, "salsafied" Hispanic elements are malleable and "morph"-able, daily demonstrating the flexibility and power of SalsaSpeak.

Meaning…and the "Private Joke"

But ours is an ironic age as well, and the absurdity of this contradiction hasn't gone completely unnoticed.

It is, in fact, a kind of "Private Joke" that most everyone knows, and that also helps to flavor the spicy use of some Hispanic elements.

Here, too, *meaning* is created, the kind of meaning that offers up the Hispanic world as an ever-present prop for whatever particular purpose one has in mind. This is Hispanic culture as The Great Hispanic Grab Bag, and part of the "joke" is that things that meant one thing in the past could just as easily mean something else in the future—without lessening the resonance of the original significance, when that is again called for.

Perhaps the best example of what one is capable of plucking out of the Great Hispanic Grab Bag—given how it started out as one of the grimmest stereotypes of Hispanics and now can capably be used for *anything* about particular people who need not be Hispanic—is the word "*macho*."

As this word has evolved in American popular culture, playing out the "Private Joke" involving Hispanics, it has given meaning and texture to the use of the Hispanic world in service to the greater good of Americans' entertainment and "salsafication."

The signal moment for "macho"—for its transition from gritty view of Hispanic men to a malleable prop in the Great Hispanic Grab Bag and a premier part of SalsaSpeak—came with the late-1970's song "Macho, Macho Man" by the group known as the "Village People."

To begin with, the group was gay, about as far from the (at the time) idea of "macho" as it was possible to go. One thing about American popular culture, it makes the world safe for parody, and the echoes of this musical send-up of a Hispanic stereotype as a source of real amusement are comfortably with us today. In the 1997 movie "In and Out," a college professor in a staid Midwestern town is rumored to be gay, and the song "Macho, macho man" is there—not only on the soundtrack, but featured in the television ads for the movie.

And, as dizzying as it is, "macho" can become (in the mind of famed talk show host Larry King of the CNN cable channel) the last best hope of America when threatened from abroad. In the wake of the tragic (and highly-publicized) school shootings over the last few years, King devoted one of his "Larry King Live" shows on CNN to the topic of possible solutions to the seeming epidemic of such shootings (by young white male students of their schools in suburban and rural areas). King balked at trying to soften the apparent natural aggression of young men, a proposal offered by one of his guests, saying it might end up endangering the country if there weren't enough "macho" defenders of our nation in the military.

The strange permutations being created by the particular meaning of Hispanics as the Fiesta People developed by pop culture have serious (and absurdly funny) implications. If Hispanics are the Salsa People, then Hispanics who speak for them are those who best represent the salsa or fiesta spirit. This would include entertainers and actors who have been (often, anyway) "selected out" for stardom because pop culture has anointed them as "icons" of "salsafying" spirit. And it would include a Mexican Chihuahua dog, famously featured in the "Taco Bell" television commercials.

But first let's look at the entertainers.

The Latino icons in show business are presented and promoted as able to spread the Hispanic spirit, to, in effect, walk among the common people and work the miracles of "conversion" to "salsafication" in their own person for non-Hispanics looking for such a miraculous change in their own spirits.

13

They are also given platforms that elected Hispanic legislators and public officials almost never get. These opportunities to "address" the American people (and to see their public utterances as having a significance that can shake one's confidence in the concept of proportionality) give the words and actions of Hispanic show business types a credence beyond their expertise on the issues in the "public policy" sphere of American life, crowding out the more pertinent statements of Hispanic elected officials, Hispanic "academics" and other more expert voices in the Hispanic community.

In this twisted logic—the operating principle for pop culture and many "opinion leaders" in American life more generally—American consumers who buy music albums from singers who offer (in their song lyrics or public pronouncements) political platitudes about including Hispanics and immigrants in American life can be thought of (can think of themselves with selfless pride) as "listening" to Hispanics and "supporting" them. Not just supporting the particular Hispanic singer, but Hispanic people in general, on whose behalf— and from whose spirit—the Hispanic singer is "speaking."

This is no stretch of the imagination when one looks at what is actually happening, what appears to be *accelerating*, in America.

Gloria Estefan, the renowned singer and businesswoman, may be the best example of this development.

During a television concert—on CBS in recent years, introducing her "Caribbean" album—Estefan spoke briefly in support of immigrants, something favorably noted by reviewers and fans.

And her husband, Emilio Estefan, is even more of a political and social visionary.

In televised interviews over the past few years, Estefan has offered a glimpse of the future as he hopes it will unfold.

There will be a greater incorporation of Hispanic spirit and flavor in pop culture's entertainments for non-Hispanics, and a greater sense of "inclusion" for Hispanics who see their spirit and cultural elements reflected in consumer entertainments.

With this backdrop, it is practically a political act when Emilio Estefan is named head of "new artist development" for Sony—as he was in 2000—the huge conglomerate with, among other things, music interests.

If the America imagined by Estefan comes to be, Hispanics will then be full partners, in some vital way, in American life. And then everything will be all right, Estefan seems to think. Hispanics will be "represented" in the institutional life of the United States, even if the direct benefits accrue to only a small number of Hispanic entrepreneurs and performers.

These are pre-eminently political reflections, on Estefan's part, statements of vision about the future of the country, of how we will live and think about each other.

And if the careers and business endeavors of the Estefans are any clue, then their efforts to bring about a more "inclusive" America will likely mean even more non-Hispanic Americans will think of Hispanics as spicy people.

As for the Taco Bell Chihuahua, "he" (there is some question whether one of the actual dogs used in the commercials is female) has become one of the most visible *spokespersons*, so to speak, on behalf of Hispanic people, as the pop culture-generated Hispanic model is increasingly defining them.

These are examples of how the meaning of Hispanic life and culture—riding the resonance of salsafication beyond pop culture—can carry, *is* carrying, critical implications for the nation's Hispanics, and for our country as a whole.

The fact that any necessary connection between Hispanic people and Hispanic spirit—the actual need for the presence of live Hispanic human beings to mediate any individual non-Hispanic's "self-salsafication"—is being effectively severed by American pop culture (and the Hispanic people replaced by "salsafied" products and "salsafied" entertainers) means much more than it might appear.

Also being disconnected, swept aside, in America's happy expropriation of Hispanic spirit, are the problems of millions of individual Hispanic-Americans.

Pop culture builds the theoretical framework that effectively clears Hispanic concerns off the national agenda and solves the problem of "assimilation" of Hispanics into American life all at the same time.

If Hispanics are the Salsa People, and non-Hispanic Americans are eating salsa, dancing to salsa (the music) and generally enjoying the fiesta spirit and fiesta elements as never before, then Hispanics have succeeded in becoming part of the "mainstream."

As ludicrous as this is—as absurd as it sounds—it is taken as fact (or something very close to it) by many serious (and highly-placed) people in the United States today, and has become a factor in play in American social and political life.

If this is the kind of country America becomes, if this sort of vision is fully realized—and it is certainly "on track" at the present time—Hispanics will have lost something critical.

They will have lost their right—only remnants of which still remain for them today—to be regarded as ordinary. And that—as we shall see—is a lot.

Because when people are simply ordinary, they have regular needs and aspirations, dreams and ambitions. They can be treated as regular human beings.

Unfortunately, Hispanics are rapidly losing what little humanity they have under the pervasive influence of pop culture's "salsafied" version of Hispanic life.

This theme is explored throughout this book, but receives special treatment in the final chapter in the larger context of the social and political implications of America's "salsafication."

It's important, however, to mention here that the capstone of pop culture's Hispanic model—the crowning triumph of its success—is as *meaning* that can be manipulated far beyond popular culture in ways that were probably unimagined by many of the people who helped to develop this *meaning*.

Masquerading as a tribute to Hispanics and Hispanic culture—at times trumpeting an emerging Hispanic *Renaissance* in the United States—pop culture's celebration of Hispanics takes on a texture of propaganda serving national political purposes.

Just as Hispanic people are being "replaced" by the resonance of their "salsafied" spirit, Hispanics' social and political concerns are being "met" (in the minds of many people) by pop culture's celebration of Hispanics and their culture.

In the next chapter, we will look at how Americans'—non-Hispanic Americans'—confidence in the use of SalsaSpeak spearheaded by the word *fiesta* is helping create the new "Fiesta People" of America.

16

CHAPTER 2

HISPANIC RESONANCE—*SALSASPEAK* AND THE "LONG GOODBYE"

"Hasta la vista, hermano."
—Cameron Mitchell to Clark Gable in the 1955 movie "The Tall Men."

"Hasta la vista, baby."
—Arnold Schwarzenegger to (almost) everybody in the 1991 movie "Terminator 2"

Every time someone says "adios"—or derivations thereof—in an American movie, it helps say "goodbye" to Hispanics.

Figuratively speaking, that is.

Millions of Hispanic-Americans haven't disappeared, of course, but it sometimes seems as if they had in America today.

For SalsaSpeak—the use of Spanish-language and Hispanic elements to "spice up" American speech and writing—is both a richly revealing opening onto the "world" of Hispanic Resonance, and part of the "Long Goodbye" to Hispanic-Americans.

And a "salsafication" of white (and other non-Hispanic) Americans that depends on a spicy picture of Hispanic life and culture—the "Hispanic Resonance" created largely by American popular culture—couldn't work without a "language" that vividly brings this Resonance to life.

Any consideration of America's ongoing "salsafication" is incomplete without an examination of the textured way in which SalsaSpeak works.

One has to admire how SalsaSpeak—what we are here terming SalsaSpeak—has spurred the advance of absurdity represented in a spreading American "salsafication."

SalsaSpeak—of which "adios" is a favored example—is, in fact, the self-evident "proof" of how the American fascination, even

17

obsession, with "salsafying" Hispanic spirit is relentlessly moving from pop culture to political culture.

SalsaSpeak allows non-Hispanics to not only "understand" but to draw enlivening Hispanic spirit from Hispanic Resonance. Of course, the "language" of SalsaSpeak is both a verbal and visual one.

Much of SalsaSpeak—just as much of America's "salsafication"—is powered by fiesta imagery.

The fiesta is a metaphor for the organized harmonies of hedonism of Hispanic life and culture. For many non-Hispanics, this is what their "salsafication," their pursuit of it, at any rate, is all about. The idea, that is, of imaginatively entering into the sensuously-rendered harmonies of the Hispanic "world" as represented by the "fiesta spirit" and the "fiesta elements" of food (and drink), music, dance, and design.

SalsaSpeak enables non-Hispanics to manipulate the *meaning* of Hispanic Resonance, the "salsafied" picture of Hispanic life and culture, without any need for the "middleman," actual Hispanic human beings.

And it helps white (and other non-Hispanic) Americans to have the confidence to become the new Fiesta People, to transfer this Hispanic Resonance into the non-Hispanic "world" of their lives and purposes.

SalsaSpeak culminates in white (and other non-Hispanic) Americans able to build their own SalsaSpeak phrases or adaptations and to (in their own mind, on some subliminal level) bid "adios" to actual Hispanic people as a necessary source of SalsaSpeak.

For every time someone, a non-Hispanic "someone," says "adios" to a non-Hispanic friend or acquaintance who answers with an "adios"—not an unheard-of occurrence in contemporary American life—they're saying goodbye to Hispanics...

And popular culture has been saying goodbye for a long time. Most everybody, it seems, has caught on by now, to the underlying principle of pop culture's SalsaSpeak for non-Hispanics. Feel a little spicy Hispanic spirit. Do it without the need for actual Hispanics to mediate the process.

Hispanic Resonance is still there, stronger than ever, but Hispanic people have been cut out of the practice of SalsaSpeak.

SalsaSpeak can be molded to the purpose at hand, since the important action—the "transfer" of "salsafied" Hispanic meaning inhering in SalsaSpeak to the non-Hispanic world—has been accomplished.

It's clear from the perspective offered over time, that all those times in the movies—"Westerns" or otherwise—when a character uses SalsaSpeak he (or she) is helping to render Hispanics ever more irrelevant.

SalsaSpeak offers certain practical, and even "political," benefits to non-Hispanics living in a country with millions of Hispanics, many of whom feel more comfortable communicating in Spanish than in English.

Thus, SalsaSpeak is so conveniently, so cleverly, a "solution" to the "language question" in America posed by all these Spanish-Speaking Hispanics here (and in the world) that it is practically a political act.

Suddenly, through SalsaSpeak, one has not only added an entirely new "language" to one's linguistic repertoire, but has "aced" the "problem" of communicating with any or all of these millions of Hispanics who speak Spanish.

For SalsaSpeak has the appearance, the *sound*, of Spanish (including *some* actual Spanish-language words) even if it doesn't exactly have the substance of the full Spanish language—despite having added "o's" and "a's" with abandon to the ends of English-language words, a regular practice in SalsaSpeak.

Obviously, no thinking person would actually believe that SalsaSpeak substitutes for Spanish. But this is what gives it the same quality of the "Private Joke" mentioned in the first chapter. It was there offered as the sardonic realization by non-Hispanic Americans of the inherent contradiction (the "Private Joke" thus shared by millions) of celebrating Hispanics-As-The-Fiesta-People on the basis of the same fundamental stereotypes used to dismiss them as brutish and emotional.

The first and foremost part of the Hispanic Resonance being transferred to non-Hispanic lives these days, of course, is encapsulated in the word "fiesta," which is helping to power the "salsafication" of non-Hispanic Americans everywhere.

But Hispanic Resonance is much broader than the word "fiesta" and the idea of Hispanics-As-The-Fiesta-People. It is a Resonance that includes the flip side of the "fiesta," Hispanics-As-Not-The-Fiesta-People, who have, to put it charitably, *too much* spicy Hispanic spirit for their own good.

When transferred to more rational, non-Hispanic Americans, however, spicy Hispanic spirit becomes an entirely different matter.

In the spirit of a responsible non-Hispanic human being, the Hispanic fiesta spirit can thrive, can find a good and abiding "home."

We will deal in this chapter with the *fiesta*, and how its *meaning* has become more easily manipulated over time for non-Hispanic uses.

And we will also look at how America's "salsafication" is bold enough—*boisterous* enough, really—to encompass the non-fiesta aspects of Hispanic Resonance (as developed largely by American popular culture over many decades) in the transfer of Hispanic *meaning* to non-Hispanic people and contexts.

Between these polar opposites of Hispanics-As-The-Fiesta-People and Hispanics-As-*Not*-The-Fiesta-People, there is, of course, a highly evocative Hispanic world (of the senses and emotions, principally) defined and delineated by SalsaSpeak.

This is primarily a world of the imagination, and if it knows any bounds, it may be only the limits of the applications to which "salsafied" Hispanic Resonance can be brought to bear.

Clearly, we have passed the point at which SalsaSpeak was largely confined to particular uses in pop culture (like "Western" movies) and reached the point at which average Americans feel familiar enough with SalsaSpeak (as "consumers" of SalsaSpeak in our pop and "political" cultures) to give it an even wider currency.

The power of Hispanic Resonance—how plainly it is presented as *meaning* for non-Hispanic lives—occasionally becomes compellingly clear in American life, as clear as the urgency of a 911 emergency call, as we will shortly see.

In fact, as Americans, we are expected—in the actual practice of popular culture and in American life more generally—to understand our life in the United States as mediated, in part, by Hispanic Resonance...

The highly publicized school shootings of recent years have been notable not only because of *where* they occurred (in rural and suburban schools) but because of *who* was committing them, namely, young white males. But in at least one of them—the Jonesboro, Arkansas school shooting in 1998—there was a Hispanic connection, of a sort. When it came time to convey the desperate urgency of the situation at "Westside School," one woman's 911 call was a plaintive plea phrased in the words of a "Western" where the cavalry is being summoned to fight the Indians: *We need help "Pronto."*

In rural Arkansas, in Jonesboro, a place not ordinarily considered a center of Hispanic life and culture—at a moment when the demands of death and the desire to prevent more of it at a middle school in the town excised all extravagance and extraneousness from the need to communicate—the automatic, the reflexive, the instinctive, took over and came up with "Pronto," a grisly lesson in the power and reach of Hispanic Resonance.

Even in Jonesboro, Arkansas, SalsaSpeak has entered American thought and speech in more than superficial ways, becoming ingrained in consciousness and available for everyday use—including a day when the unspeakable happened far from violence-plagued urban centers of America.

Hispanic Resonance as American Cultural History—A Life Reduced to Resonance

There is an elegiac quality about Hispanic Resonance in America's *Story*, in the unfolding, ongoing story of our country.

When Broadway (and Hollywood) lost one of its own on Oct. 18, 2000 with the death of actress Gwen Verdon, the obituaries gave more than a glimpse of this elegy, this homage to Hispanic Resonance, at work.

Verdon was remembered in her death notices as a variety of Hispanic Resonance, her life made notable largely because of her role as "Lola" in the musical "Damn Yankees."

Here's how the Associated Press, the massive global news service, had it in the opening line of its Verdon obituary, as published in the Oct. 19, 2000 edition of the *Washington* (D.C.) *Times* newspaper.

21

"Gwen Verdon, Broadway's premier female dancer who was the seductive Lola in 'Damn Yankees'…died yesterday at 75."

In the Oct. 19, 2000 edition of the Washington Post, Verdon's obituary said, in part, "She would forever be identified with the vampish Lola in the 1955 musical 'Damn Yankees.'"

The character of "Lola" was parody playing off parody, a sendup of the (at the time) more closely contemporaneous character of Carmen Miranda, portrayed by the actress of the same name.

Most famous, perhaps, for her fruit bowl hats, Miranda showed how a Hispanic accent, a little rhythm and lively songs could evoke a powerful "re-creation" of a happy Hispanic world, a fiesta of the spirit.

This happy daydream of Hispanic life and culture could be satirized at the same time it was being celebrated for its pungency of human spirit, for its punchy rendering of personality in the character of "Lola."

If this is not exactly what people who see the movie on television or on videotape—or local productions of the musical—take away from the experience, it was a subtlety realized by the obituary writers chronicling the *contribution* of Verdon to the world.

It was a contribution to Hispanic Resonance, to its development and popularization, an expansion, in effect, of what it means to be an American.

As is clear from the movie in which Verdon also starred—a fitting capstone to her portrayal of "Lola" in the presentation of the musical on Broadway—Verdon did seem to have an intuitive sense of the delicious ironies involved in the role.

The plot revolves around a finely honed realization of Hispanic Resonance and the possibilities for the parody of it, a remarkable achievement in the cultural history of America considering the less ironic time at which it appeared.

For Verdon is not *really* "Lola," the Latin seductress. This is simply one of her *personas*, employed, as needed, in her work for The Devil. She is clearly, as the bare description of her character in the musical might read, a beautiful woman. But she has only become so by the mystical intervention of the Devil (played in the movie by Ray Walston), who has transformed her from her original state and station as "the ugliest woman in *Providence*, Rhode Island," to her newly beatific appearance.

Her new assignment—early on in the movie—is to help her employer take the "soul" of a middle-aged man who has (through the good offices of Walston) temporarily become a virile young baseball player leading his team on a winning path, on track to defeat the "Damn Yankees."

But the bargain made between the aging man from Hannibal, Missouri, and the Devil offering major-league baseball immortality is fraying like the seams of, well, a worn baseball.

Joe, the man, misses his wife. The Devil, on the other hand, is steaming because Joe has an "escape clause" in the "contract" to give his soul to the Devil.

The solution: Bring in "Lola." She'll make Joe forget about his long-suffering wife, who loves Joe after years of married life as much as she did on the day they were married and waits patiently for him on the porch of their modest house, sitting close to the rocking chair that was Joe's favorite.

Actually, to be precise, Verdon has some latitude (in the plot of the musical) about which of her sexy guises to use.

But she finally decides to "put on"—much as the decision about what clothes to wear—her "Lola" persona.

Verdon thus became one of the more famous examples of the proposition—proven over and over by American popular culture over time—that Hispanic Resonance can be effectively used by non-Hispanics.

And while she may or may not have lived an exemplary life in all respects, she certainly led an *exemplar* life, in the sense of personifying Hispanic Resonance.

"Damn Yankees" is noteworthy in our explanation of Hispanic Resonance, especially because it demonstrates our willing suspension of reality about Hispanic life and culture in our eagerness to enjoy the Hispanic daydream.

And whatever Verdon may have thought about her life, in her final years, the obituary writers summarized its supposed significance in this very particular way.

Hispanic Resonance as "Self-Help" Therapy—"Don Juan DeMarco"

The character known as "Don Juan" becomes elevated—much as the ongoing "celebration" of Hispanics these days lifts the trivializing stereotypes of Hispanics-As-The-Fiesta-People into a "tribute" to them—in the exercise of *applied* Hispanic Resonance.

The "Latin Lover" stereotype—the male counterpart of the Latin seductress exemplified by "Lola"—comes to be seen as taking us by the hand to lead us to a higher, more spiritual place in the movie "Don Juan DeMarco" starring Johnny Depp and Marlon Brando.

This is impressive, indeed, given the long history of pop culture practice in the United States regarding the idea of "Don Juan."

It is a dizzying, or maybe heady, experience. For the exultation—apparent in the clear exhilaration felt by many non-Hispanic Americans in their "self-salsafication" from Hispanic Resonance—appears to be genuine enough.

And much of the liberating spirit from SalsaSpeak does seem to center on the highly malleable nature (in actual American practice) of SalsaSpeak and the resonance of the Hispanic "world" it permits.

In this 1995 film, Faye Dunaway is desperately grateful to "Don Juan"—Johnny Depp's incarnation of him, anyway—for triggering the transformation of her husband, played by Brando.

Brando has been neglecting Dunaway for years, emotionally speaking, and she has been *waiting*, as she finally tells Brando, for him to see the error of his ways.

The movie doesn't deal with the question that springs to mind about *why* Dunaway hasn't told Brando sometime before, during all those years when he was neglecting her, that she was incredibly unhappy.

Depp (in the movie) has come with no identity, and no discernible past.

Brando comes to a realization that Depp is saner than most people, has a healthier, more "integrated" personality than a majority of "normal" people.

The screenwriter, speaking on behalf of society, is saying, in effect, *all the time we were using "Don Juan" to help put down*

Hispanics, we were just playing. We see how "Don Juan" is really a lesson for us about what's important.

This movie is a signal event in "The Long Goodbye" to Hispanics, a heartfelt wave goodbye.

It is a significant example of how the foundation of Hispanic Resonance can be creatively molded to new, non-Hispanic purposes.

The clear message of the movie is a clarion call to us all to reconfigure our view of the world and ourselves.

Worse the luck we don't all have a "Don Juan" in our lives, as Example to Show Us a Better Way, a more enlightened vision of life and the day-to-day consummation of our engagement with all it offers.

Far from being a respectful nod to Hispanics, however, this elasticized evocation of a Hispanic character is profoundly demeaning.

Beyond the fact this character has been used to portray Hispanics in a negative light—and in "Don Juan DeMarco" is only being spruced up in order to add (or evoke) a more spiritual dimension of Hispanic Resonance for use by non-Hispanics in their individual "self-salsafications"—there is the fact that Hispanic Resonance as applied to actual Hispanic human beings is rarely as uplifting in the practice of American life.

Although Johnny Depp is not the whitest white person on the planet—and of course there are some Hispanics who are light-skinned since Hispanics, as a group, come in all races and complexions—he is certainly not a Hispanic, but has nonetheless become a living embodiment of a Hispanic "Don Juan."

He speaks with his version of a Spanish accent, dresses in what he imagines to be the way a historical "Don Juan" would've dressed, and practices swordplay right there at the insane asylum.

It helps that the place where Depp practices *looks* like a Spanish design, a courtyard atop one of the levels of the mental institution, to which one can look down from another level of the building, an open-air dining area where Brando gazes down upon Depp wielding a sword against imaginary opponents and contemplates this unusual case.

"I Love Lucy"

You know something's wrong with the idea of a highly amplified Hispanic "influence" in the United States when much of this "influence" comes from the "I Love Lucy" Show.

And you know that this "influence" is not the best one to represent Hispanic-Americans when—despite Lucille Ball's direction to the writers at the time never to negatively portray the character of "Ricky Ricardo"—the show ridicules "Ricky's" Cuban accent, Latin music, and Hispanic culture generally.

But perhaps more than any other Hispanic "influence" in American popular culture, the "I Love Lucy" Show has profoundly affected American life.

The "I Love Lucy" Show allowed white (and other non-Hispanic) Americans to become familiar with Hispanic Resonance, showed them how this Resonance could be navigated and nuanced.

It helped (and helps, in reruns) non-Hispanic Americans see Hispanic Resonance as malleable "material" which can be used for their own purposes.

In recent years, this has been revealed in sometimes surprising ways.

For Hispanic Resonance—and the SalsaSpeak that vividly calls it to mind—is available to anyone for anything, for any purpose.

Conservative commentator and former presidential candidate Patrick Buchanan (on the Reform Party ticket in 2000) has, to put it mildly, some concerns about the value of Hispanic immigration to the United States. In his most recent book—"The Death of the West" published in late 2001—Buchanan says Hispanic immigrants are putting America at risk as a nation with one language and culture. But Buchanan appears to have no such problem with Hispanic *Resonance*. On the "Larry King Live" show on CNN just weeks before the November 2000 election, Buchanan made a point by prefacing it with the idea of having to "splain" something like, Buchanan said, "Ricky Ricardo" would say.

As a skilled communicator with wide experience—ranging from White House speechwriter to (former) co-host of a public-affairs television program, "Crossfire" on CNN—Buchanan can obviously be viewed as someone who chooses his words judiciously (perhaps especially when he is being injudicious, or deliberately provocative).

He is certainly aware—as his own employment of it shows—of the communicative currency in America these days of citing "Ricky Ricardo" using "splain" (or "splaining") as ammunition for one's own linguistic endeavors.

And Buchanan presumably knows a little something about his potential audience, of their "knowledge" and expectations in this regard.

There is a more important lesson of the "I Love Lucy" phenomenon than the one about how broad-minded white Americans were to accept in the 1950's the premise of a show involving a "mixed" marriage, a fact noted in books and documentaries about the program.

The more germane lesson is how adaptable Americans (including white and other non-Hispanic Americans) are when it comes to being entertained.

And why white Americans felt the need to be so adaptable, to bring the exotic and (even) erotic echoes of Hispanic Resonance into everyday American life.

This is the idea of how something is not only missing, typically at least, in non-Hispanic American life, but is something to be missed, to long for and desire.

The sense of the distinctive difference of Hispanic spirit and sensation—the animating essence of Hispanic Resonance—from white American spirit and life is at work here.

The writers of the "I Love Lucy" Show effectively used, effectively *created*, SalsaSpeak material in order to evoke Hispanic Resonance of the time and to extend it, certainly. So successful were they that non-Hispanic Americans have been able to use the show specifically for all kinds of purposes not contemplated (it is probably safe to say) by them. As in the aforementioned example of Pat Buchanan, for instance.

Some Hispanics may find a reassurance in this Resonance.

These Hispanics may—on some level of consciousness—feel "well, at least they're thinking of us in an affectionate way" by their (white Americans') fondness for the "Ricky Ricardo" character.

The ability of Hispanic Resonance to substitute for the educative work of what has come to be widely known as "multiculturalism" is a remarkable one.

Non-Hispanic Americans can, without necessarily having had any direct contact with Hispanics, *apply* this "knowledge" as *meaning*.

The fluency with which white (and other non-Hispanic) Americans wield their "knowledge" of Hispanics (in the United States and elsewhere) suggests how successful Hispanic Resonance—as promulgated by popular culture and other influences in American life—has been.

This certainly appears to be the expectation of those who seek to directly use the resonant *meaning* of the "I Love Lucy" show.

This idea is codified in the "Think Different" ad campaign for "Apple Computer" Company.

For this ad—which simply featured a picture of Lucille Ball and Desi Arnaz (the "Lucy and Ricky" of the "I Love Lucy" show) with the words "Think Different"—"Apple" was simply taking note of what white (and other non-Hispanic) Americans had done in watching the "I Love Lucy" show.

You were thinking differently, in a more open-minded way, when you saw the "I Love Lucy" show and accepted the unusual premise (at the time) of a Hispanic man and white woman as a happily married couple despite their obvious differences.

The delightful irony here is how the ethnic differences between "Lucy" and "Ricky" (paralleled in real life for the time they were married) were probably the *least* of their differences as characters.

And if this is one of the layers of consciousness—or the main one—brought to mind among non-Hispanic Americans by the Apple Computer ad, all to the good, as far as Apple is concerned.

The important thing—for Apple—is for people to apply this same understanding and acceptance of difference to a vision of technology, or more precisely, the kinds of innovative, or "different" computer technologies offered by Apple.

The communication of all this, the connective strands tying all the sequences of conscious (or subconscious) thinking processes together, is so spare because it rests on an (entirely valid) expectation of how Hispanic Resonance has helped condition us.

For a time in the 1990's the Green Bay Packers professional football team featured the "Three Amigos," three players (including quarterback Brent Fahre and tight end Mark Chmura) who had so named themselves. And if—like the example of Pat Buchanan using "splain"—the extraordinary example of three non-Hispanic football players in *Wisconsin* being "warmed" by self-styling themselves as "The Three Amigos" borders on the bizarre, it is yet more evidence of the power of Hispanic Resonance.

These are, arguably, men who have explicitly felt the resonance of fame in a way relatively few other people, relatively *few other professional football players*, ever have. They were in two consecutive "Super Bowls" in the 1990's, winning one of them.

And yet they found a vital Resonance—reveled in this personal "declaration of self-salsafication"—in the use of SalsaSpeak.

Green Bay, Wisconsin—like Jonesboro, Arkansas—is not a center of Hispanic population or culture in the United States, but it became for a time in the 1990's one of the centers of *Hispanic Resonance*, as the key offensive players of the city's professional football team (the "Three Amigos") led the team to these back-to-back Super Bowl appearances.

The Resonance of "Fiesta"

> "When I use a word," Humpty Dumpty said, in rather a scornful tone, "it means just what I choose it to mean—nothing more nor less."
>
> "The question is," said Alice, "whether you can make words mean so many different things."
>
> "The question is," said Humpty Dumpty, "which is to be master—that's all."
>
> —**Alice in Wonderland** by Lewis Carroll.

The exuberance of Hispanic Resonance—as we see in the current, *constant* celebration of Hispanic culture in American life—quickens apace at the very mention of the word "fiesta." This is a Hispanic Resonance being actively "downloaded" for use in non-Hispanic contexts and purposes.

Fiesta has become synonymous with fun for many white (and other non-Hispanic) people, even when the activity in question has nothing to do with Hispanics or Hispanic elements.

And if you're not having a *fiesta* you're not having any fun, the theory appears to be.

The word *fiesta* has an edge, an energy, which the word "fun" no longer seems to have.

And for the new Fiesta People, non-Hispanic people who have the affluence and exuberance to embody a kind of generalized fiesta spirit not necessarily restricted to the Hispanic spirit or Hispanic elements, the word "fiesta" is indispensable. Of course, even as this newer, non-Hispanic extension of the term *fiesta* becomes ever more diffused and ever more pervasive in our popular culture, the connection to the *resonance* of the Hispanic world by virtue of the word *fiesta* is undeniable.

And, to be precise, the fiestas of white (and other non-Hispanic) people very often do have the Hispanic spirit and Hispanic elements directly in mind, even if the "middleman"—Hispanic people—is missing. But not, apparently, missed.

The poignancy of Americans' apparent longing for "salsafied" Hispanic spirit—and for the hedonistic Hispanic harmonies symbolized by the word "fiesta"—may have been completely captured a few years ago in, of all things, a restaurant review in *BackStage*," an entertainment newspaper published in New York City.

The review was headlined "Poco Loco: A Fiesta in Midtown," and opened with these words, "Visitors entering Poco Loco, a new Mexican restaurant…may feel like they've stumbled onto a fiesta."

What seemed especially intriguing about the review (in the July 10, 1992 issue of *BackStage*) was the fact that it—like the newspaper—was directed to readers who (as "show business" *types*) help enliven the spirits of others.

Of course, their spirit—even the actors among them who must have some extra spark of spirit in order to do what they do—has to be attended to as well.

And this idea, too, seemed to emerge: The Fiesta Spirit is quite capable of recharging one, even when one is already a normally spirited person.

This is how powerful fiesta spirit is, the review appeared to say.

And when fiesta spirit is this important, it can't be left to chance that one will stumble into it in mid-town Manhattan.

For, among other reasons, no matter how big New York City is, it is not home to all Americans.

The Fiesta Spirit must be made available to all, in the United States certainly, and eventually the world.

Wherever one is, whatever one is doing, the perfect realization of the fiesta spirit must be made possible, and American ingenuity is proving itself up to the task.

In the 1997 movie "Breakdown," starring Kurt Russell and Kathleen Quinlan as husband-and-wife, the couple is traveling in the middle of the desert, somewhere in the American Southwest.

It couldn't be more desolate, with few other cars to be seen on the highway as they drive along, and only the desert to be seen on either side of the highway.

They finally find a place to stop briefly—a gasoline station. And while Russell fills up the car with gas, Quinlan goes into the station's mini-mart to buy a few snack items.

Back on the road, the couple has the following conversation…

"What'd you get?" Russell asks.

"Let's see…junk-food 'fiesta,'" Quinlan replies.

And so, even in the middle of the desert, a couple in a car traveling down the highway are able to participate in and partake of the Hispanic fiesta spirit—and by extension, the non-Hispanics viewing the movie are also able to participate in this suffused fiesta spirit.

If the idea of "excess" is involved here—as it seems to be—one can see the evolution of language, of the American language, unfolding. On the MTV cable channel a couple of years later, in 1999, any subtlety is shorn, when MTV host John Norris (on a special program examining the history of Spring Break) describes Spring Break as an exercise in "fiesta excess." But what is more significant is how the fiesta spirit is there for Americans, non-Hispanic Americans, whenever they wish to summon it. The *compartmentalization* of American life is obviously in play. And the easy way in which a couple driving through the desert can suddenly import the fiesta spirit to freshen the long drive exemplifies pop culture's use of the fiesta resonance when needed.

And, at the moment it is invoked in "Breakdown," it is certainly needed. We can almost hear Quinlan, the *character* played by Quinlan, thinking to herself...*Time for a fiesta...Need one now. No better time. Out in the middle of nowhere.*

Of course, there is always the "Ford Fiesta" automobile. Maybe then—as in the "Breakdown" movie scene—one could *really* feel whatever one was doing in the car to be a fiesta.

The ability to summon the spirit of the fiesta, even in the unlikely setting of desert desolation—like calling forth the genie in a tale of the Arabian Nights—seems magical. And this magic—like a wish granted by genie in one of those wonderful tales—acts, or can, as artificial respiration for an entire country, infusing the spirit of the fiesta into American life.

The resonance of the fiesta—powering pop culture use of Hispanic elements and average Americans' "self-salsafication"—relies on the boundless power of the imagination to create a reality of sorts about something that is, for most non-Hispanic Americans, outside of their actual experience.

Outside their actual life experience of a Hispanic fiesta, but not, certainly not, outside the power of their imaginative projection and apparent longing.

The word *fiesta* spearheads the currently most popular use of Hispanic Resonance, the celebration of Hispanics for their contribution of piquant spirit and fiesta elements like food and music to the nation's non-Hispanics.

The *fiesta* has given a renewed vigor to Hispanic Resonance, one that encompasses the entire Hispanic world.

And one that gives many non-Hispanic Americans a *reason* to do things in their own lives that are much more serious than the simple enjoyment of fiesta spirit and fiesta elements.

Like higher education, for example.

Hispanic Resonance here shows how evocative and enticing its fiesta strains can be.

On its website, George Washington University (located, appropriately enough, in Washington, D.C.) helps potential applicants to its "Study Abroad" program in Spain with "links" to the "Lonely Planet" guide to Spain.

"Lonely Planet" begins its introduction to Spain thusly, "The exuberance of the Spaniards and the glorious predictability of the summer weather have been attracting refugees from northern Europe's damp and clammy lands for decades..."

These are clearly people you can *party* with, and with weather (certainly during the summer) conducive to *fiestas*.

Hispanics are not only seen as being attuned to their spirit, but also (no small feat) with a spirit worth being attuned to.

The *essentiality* of this feeling cannot be overemphasized.

The idea of Hispanics as Fiesta People plays off the very definite sense of them as simple enough, childlike really, to be satisfied by sensory pleasures. This incredibly stereotyped view of Hispanics gets glossed-over (obviously) in the "positive" reformulation of Hispanics-As-Fiesta-People. Part of the urge among non-Hispanics to draw what they see (what pop culture has *helped them to see*) as enlivening Hispanic spirit from Hispanic people is based on the idea of radically simplifying one's life.

Even if only for a short time, one can forget about one's more complicated interior life of the mind, can leave one's *organization* of rational thought processes behind and venture, through imaginative projection, into the Hispanic world intuited by feeling.

The obvious point to be made here, the one so obviously not made in the popular media, is that a genuine interest in and respect for authentic Hispanic culture would signify an interest in and respect for actual Hispanic human beings.

One would be interested in their harmonies, presumably reached through the same Hispanic spirit and elements in which non-Hispanics seem to find such practical and artistic aesthetic harmonies.

The easy evolution of fiesta meaning is a kind of playful competition by creative people in advertising, among other places, off the same set of ideas and images of Hispanics as the Salsa or Fiesta People, and the ongoing transfer of their fiesta or salsa spirit to non-Hispanic people.

And its relentless development by pop culture lends itself to useful categories like...

Fastest connection between "salsa" the hot sauce and the idea of a "fiesta"—And the Winner Is...a September 2000 commercial for Pepcid AC. In the commercial, a black couple is shopping in a supermarket, with the man occasionally stopping to taste the free food samples offered by marketers staffing tables in the store set up for just this purpose.

As the man spies a "Salsa" food table with an inviting display of salsa picante sauce in a large container and tortilla chips on the side, he says with almost gleeful anticipation, "Fiesta Time."

Shortly after he has enjoyed this "fiesta," however, tummy troubles begin and the man has to be helped by a relieving dose of Pepcid AC.

The man soon feels better and is once again ready for future fiestas.

Even if the salsa exhibited in the spot was not authentic, something was genuinely going on here.

The advance in meaning—the *accelerating* advance of fiesta meaning—is clearly evident.

What is immediately intelligible to *consumers* (of the ideas involved, first of all) is the tie-in between the sensory sensation and satisfaction of eating salsa and the emotional enjoyment of Hispanic fiesta spirit, the exhilaration actual Hispanics would be feeling if they were eating the salsa.

This is becoming so obvious over time in American popular culture it almost seems ridiculous to point it out. But if any people are pointing it out, their voices are being muted in the media by the "celebration" of Hispanic fiesta elements and spirit.

Even more significantly, of course, the rapid inroads of such a Hispanic resonance into political analysis and public policy debates also appear to be overlooked. And these are the more troubling aspects of the pop culture-generated ideas of "salsafied" Hispanic life and culture.

Popular culture has been moving in this direction for a long time now.

In the 1956 Western movie "The Proud Ones," a Mexican *bandito* praises his Anglo host (who has called in the bandit to help in the "contract" killing of the sheriff) for offering him "Amontillado" wine.

"Ah, Senor, you have a Spanish soul," the bandito says admiringly.

The SalsaSpeak shorthand is crystal clear here. Tangible Hispanic elements, *fiesta elements*, like food and drink, are expressive of and productive of "salsafied" Hispanic spirit.

The Hispanic "world" is intuited, understood at its most elemental level, by reference to sensory sensations and emotional resonance. And if one, as a non-Hispanic, is properly appreciative of all this, one can be properly seen as having empathy, understanding of Hispanic life and culture—even to the point of being an "honorary" Hispanic. Or of having a "Spanish soul," as the Latin character in "The Proud Ones" says.

Of course, once this secret is out, as is so clearly the case in the massively scaled "salsafication" of America, there is *really* no need for actual Hispanic-American people.

This is an idea we will examine in some depth in the next chapter, on the "Sensory Search," namely, how the new, non-Hispanic Fiesta People make the conversion complete by the sensory sensation of the Hispanic fiesta elements of food (and drink), music, dance and design.

SalsaSpeak is thus the first step on the "food chain" of Hispanic Resonance.

And there really seems to be something to this, to this incorporation of fiesta spirit into the lifestyles of people who aren't able to avail themselves of more geographically-conducive means (the proximity to parts of the country like the Southwest) of experiencing Hispanic elements and harmonies.

The evolution of this single term explains better than anything else, perhaps, how the transfer of Hispanic spirit from Hispanic to non-Hispanic people has been accomplished.

It's instructive, too, in understanding the increasing irrelevance of Hispanic human beings in America today and the continuing damage being done to our American language and to our very perception.

Early demonstrations of this "transfer" of Hispanic spirit to the non-Hispanics among us are somehow both poignant and pathetic.

The Great Depression

At roughly the same time that tens of thousands of undocumented Mexican (and other Latino) workers in the United States were being forcibly deported to Mexico, an America in the throes of the Great Depression was taking some comfort from Hispanic spirit.

The pool of such spirit in the United States had been somewhat lessened by the expatriation of all those Hispanics, but the metaphorical manipulation of Hispanic spirit allows of some incongruity with reality.

A pair of examples from the 1930's illustrates the dual paths the fiesta has taken in American popular culture—the first in what may be termed the "strict constructionist" view and the other representative of the "transformational" tradition.

Although these examples are *not* claimed here as the *first* instances of such usages in American pop culture as an absolutely historical beginning of the chronology in question, they are notable steps along the way to the present moment.

We begin with Gene Autry, the "Singing Cowboy" who made dozens of movies and whose signal contribution to the developing SalsaSpeak of the Depression-era pop culture came with the song "South of the Border." The lyrics of the song—featured in the Autry movie entitled, appropriately enough, "South of the Border"—include the line "...South of the Border, Down Mexico Way, That's where I fell in love...but it was *fiesta* (italics added) and our hearts were gay..."

Autry effectively creates an evocative (and empathetic) setting of a Mexican fiesta and fiesta spirit from explicitly Hispanic roots.

This is a place, and a feeling, in which one can—as a non-Hispanic, as Autry is—happily lose oneself for a time. "...But it was *fiesta*..." thus becomes an *explanation*, a reason for falling in love, even though—as in the morning after awakening from a "one-night stand" with a beguiling stranger—one realizes that reality must take precedence.

In the other, "transformational" example, we see an early instance of the *applied* resonance of *fiesta* taken from the Hispanic world and used to enliven a non-Hispanic use with SalsaSpeak.

In hindsight, of course, the introduction to the world of "Fiesta Ware" dinnerware—plates, bowls, and pitchers, among other items—in the midst of the Great Depression was the shape, so to speak, of things to come.

Any quick search of the Internet reveals how richly any early investment in "Fiesta Ware" has paid off.

But we are concerned here with the "investment" America has made in fiesta resonance (and Hispanic Resonance more generally).

As long ago as the 1930's—when the social climate for Hispanics was far less sympathetic than it is today, even given the exceptions that can certainly be cited in contemporary America—the resonance of the Hispanic fiesta could play a poignant (or pathetic) part in helping lift the spirits of average Americans desperately in need of just such a boost.

But, as we've noted, the particular ways in which this Hispanic Resonance is employed, and the *meaning* drawn from them, can differ markedly.

In the Autry example, the medium of the movies—what movies typically *do*—helps to render of the fiesta a vicarious experience for the non-Hispanics seeing the picture (and hearing the song in question) in its original release (and ever since, of course, as a television rerun, or more recently on videotape).

It is, metaphorically speaking, a pleasant place to visit, but *we couldn't live there.*

The "FiestaWare" example offers a radically different rendering of the world and our psychological empowerment. We *can* have the fiesta—its spirit, at least, for this is what is most important about the fiesta—residing with us, in some fashion.

American popular culture has been doing its level best to prove the power of this proposition, in what can only be described as a wildly accelerating effort in the last few years in the "FiestaWare" mold, figuratively speaking.

It must be said here (or said again, for the implication is likely already clear) that Autry has played a large part over the years—"South of the Border" being one of the best-known "Hispanic" songs in American popular culture—in deepening the Hispanic Resonance so vital to the success of the applied, or "transformational" types of Hispanic Resonance exemplified early on by "FiestaWare."

As we've just seen, the magic of Hispanic Resonance—in the hands of creative people—resides in the way it can be reshaped to fit any purpose, be it the selling of dinnerware, cowboy movies, or, in the last few decades, a football game (the annual "Fiesta Bowl" in Arizona).

It helps, is *critical*, to the "salsafication" of non-Hispanic Americans from Hispanic sensation and spirit.

At its best, SalsaSpeak evokes a vivid resonance of the Hispanic "world." This is a spirit heightened by the piquant immediacy of direct sensory sensation of Hispanic food, music, dance, and design (like bright colors)—all the elements of the "fiesta."

And in the next chapter—the <u>Sensory Search</u> for a Hispanic-based "salsafication"—we will look at how resonance links up with direct sensory sensation.

SalsaSpeak allows us to not only intuit Hispanic harmonies—like the "fiesta"—but also Hispanic hierarchies, including those in the built environment.

The Hispanic-flavored designs of, say, "Chi Chi's" chain Mexican restaurants are saying something very specific, albeit in a summary fashion.

There is a harmony herein, highlights conveniently and affordably offered of the harmonies one would find in the Hispanic "world" of one's imagination. As our collective imagination has been tutored to envision such a Hispanic world, that is.

(We will take a more detailed look in the next chapter at "Chi Chi's" efforts to offer an experience of the Hispanic "world.")

"Chi Chi's" and other chain Mexican restaurants—including the nearly 6, 700 "Taco Bells" in the United States—are an important part of SalsaSpeak imagery taking tangible form in the built environment.

But there is a lot that SalsaSpeak and Hispanic Resonance can do before we "join" the fiesta in "progress" in America by checking in with "Chi Chi's" chain Mexican restaurants in the next chapter.

We can, for example, *talk* about tacos before we take the time (and take up the *meaning* of the <u>Sensory Search</u> in the next chapter) to *have* some actual tacos.

And what can we talk about, when it comes to tacos, and other tangible Hispanic items?

Well, there is irony, as delicious (and for many people, even more so) on one level as the actual experience of eating tacos and other Latin food items.

And "setting the table" here for our (at times) sumptuous SalsaSpeak "feast" of tasty Hispanic elements for an experience of "food for thought" is another part of SalsaSpeak, built on imagery.

The "**Dreamscape**" *of Visual SalsaSpeak*

SalsaSpeak offers a rich visual component, a *dreamscape*, for our vicarious ventures into the "salsafied" Hispanic world, in commercials, movies, television, and even print advertisements. The shorthand of SalsaSpeak is increasingly supplemented by this summary visual "language" of Hispanic life and culture.

By repetition and nuance, this visual rendering of Hispanic Resonance can be effectively evocative of the simplified, spicy idea of the Hispanic world promulgated by pop culture.

Of course, relying on *resonance*, on the evocative sense of something more substantial, works just as well as far as pop culture is concerned—and as far as many people (more, probably, than reasonable people might want to believe) are concerned.

The shortcut from Hispanic reality to Hispanic resonance so often taken by American pop culture—and others "outside" pop culture that play off it for their own purposes—is aided by the (at times) sense in the "popular imagination" of the Hispanic "world" as dream.

In a world increasingly mediated by image, where the images chosen in, say, a commercial have only seconds to do their work, visual SalsaSpeak becomes all-important.

Fiesta imagery is a central part of visual SalsaSpeak, particularly as it offers up places seemingly uniquely created for a fiesta.

The open square set in Latin America, with the church in the background, as a place to hold a fiesta or show strolling couples, is one of the visual commonplaces in American advertising using Hispanic Resonance.

This becomes painfully obvious in commercials showing a fiesta, or some aspect of it, in order to sell us products which (presumably) contain the concentrated "extract" of fiesta spirit to enjoy with our friends or even when alone at home. But it also works to good effect in movies where this Hispanic *dreamscape* is offered with occasionally ironic or nightmarish overtones.

This kind of SalsaSpeak imagery—especially when it shows us urban landscapes remade in the wake of a demographically changing America (more Hispanics, that is)—reminds us of the actual infrastructure of "salsafication" in our country.

In movies, on television, SalsaSpeak imagery (often combined with Latin music) is as richly revelatory of the "salsafied" Hispanic world as its verbal counterpart.

Of course, as might be surmised, verbal and visual SalsaSpeak work in tandem, a "tag-team" engaged in exploiting the possibilities of Hispanic Resonance for our greater entertainment and "salsafication."

In the 1970's—and again in the 1990's with its series of made-for-television movies—the television series "The Rockford Files" starring James Garner as an amiable private investigator offered a primer in Visual SalsaSpeak.

Rockford (or Garner) was always, it seemed, eating tacos in the original television series, delighting in the often-disgusting picture this presented to some of the more refined people who had to watch him revel in a hands-on approach to the tacos while they detailed the case they wanted Rockford to take on for them.

In one of the television movies, at a moment when Rockford is clearly not enjoying the "fiesta spirit"—trying to figure out how to escape from the bad guys—he is standing in a parking lot against the backdrop of a huge sign reading "Bienvenido a Fiesta Tacos" (literally, "Welcome to 'Fiesta Tacos'").

The 1999 movie "Oxygen" is another one of the many examples of American movies that can be cited to show the "tag-team" of verbal-visual SalsaSpeak at work.

In one scene, a police detective is explaining what he has found out about a stolen car used by a kidnapper, and in the course of this description settles comfortably into SalsaSpeak, "...no prints, no witnesses, *nada...*"

In an earlier scene in the movie, a female police detective who has just wounded a suspect in a shootout walks away in a half-daze as some of her fellow officers rush in to handcuff the man and "secure" the scene. The camera lingers on the backdrop as the detective ambles off, a Latin store with a sign reading "La Pera," at which (the sign notes) "live poultry" is offered for sale.

In the *Dreamscape* of Hispanic Resonance provided by movies, Hispanic visual elements are like the architectural accents of a house suggesting Hispanic influences. Little touches, here and there, to spice up the "look" of the movie, and to update the evolving "Portrait of America" produced by films, which as one of their main functions give us a vicarious sense of traveling to (and seeing, obviously) places we might otherwise not ever see (or fail to see in the same way as the filmmaker's vision allows us to).

Visual SalsaSpeak takes on a greater importance, rides the renewed interest in the resonance of the "salsafied" Hispanic world, in movies aiming to show a contemporary *look*, a vividly rendered imagery of a changing America.

This is such a powerful influence, and so familiar to people whose "language" as filmmakers is a visual one, that it shows itself in intriguing ways. Like the 1997 movie "The Good Bad Guy," which was written and directed by Ezio Greggio, an Italian filmmaker trying his hand at an English-language American movie.

Even a foreigner like Greggio, who also stars in the movie as a petty crook forced by circumstance to "take on" the Mafia, understands the value of Visual SalsaSpeak.

The movie, a gentle parody of action films, incorporates a comic twist on SalsaSpeak and echoes of unflattering Hispanic Resonance. Greggio gets to stay at a California seaside lodging named "Mala Noche" Motel.

By its "look" and by its name (literally "bad night" in Spanish) the motel evokes (or, perhaps more precisely, reeks of) a seedy Mexican motel.

Hispanic Hierarchies of Meaning

SalsaSpeak is clearer—one's "self-salsafication" as a non-Hispanic is surer—when one "understands" the hierarchy of Hispanic harmonies.

At its best—or most hyped, whichever applies in particular cases—the happy dream fleshed out by Hispanic imagery is offered up as a realization (in which non-Hispanics can share) of the highest aesthetic harmonies of Hispanic life and culture.

The hierarchies of the Hispanic world—and their role in the use of Hispanic Resonance in the marketing of Hispanic-style products and other applications in American life—demonstrate how textured and specific the evocative Hispanic world has become over time. And it is vital—in any effort to understand how this process of ranking does its part to trivialize and distort Hispanic human beings—to examine this powerful strand of Hispanic Resonance.

The "depth" of SalsaSpeak—the degree to which it can take us on an imaginative journey to the Hispanic world—is also shown by its visual component, which provides us a glimpse into the higher Hispanic harmonies, including artistic ones.

In pop culture practice, the facile ordering of Hispanic harmonies spans the decades of American pop culture's engagement with Hispanic Resonance. The capacity for this Hispanic dream—and these harmonies—to lift one's spirits to soaring heights, is most often rendered when Spain and connections to Spain are invoked.

Spain has a purity, an aesthetic finery, which cannot be matched by any other Hispanic country (including the "nation" of Hispanics in the United States). Spain is the undisputed center of undiluted Hispanic spirit and culture, uncontaminated by the intervention and intermingling, significantly, of other peoples (blacks and native Indians) and influences in other Hispanic countries.

But Spanish Resonance reaches from the "Old World" of Spain to the "New World" of America in which the Spanish influence was, for a time, pre-eminent and still lingers.

Helped along in America, certainly, by the relentless commercial exploitation of Spanish Resonance by American popular culture.

The aesthetic artistic harmonies of Spanish art, dance and music have their counterpart in practical harmonies of ordered emotion and ethics. And here too, the highest Hispanic harmonies are found (or from) Spain…

In this regard, we must consider the image of bullfighting, and the powerful evocations of the spirit's essence that are, at root, represented by the matador, resplendent in a "suit of lights" symbolically shining from the brilliant spark of courage from within.

When one examines the genesis of this picture of the matador—and one must do so in order to understand the shorthand of SalsaSpeak imagery in comprehending hierarchies—the idea of unsullied Spanish spirit can be clearly seen.

In this "Moment of Truth"—famously phrased by Ernest Hemingway, whose writings on bullfighting are inextricably melded into our views of Spanish Resonance—the undiluted, unalloyed virtue of courage is clearly evident.

We can feel the vicarious thrill of the matador's confrontation with the bull, and ultimately, with himself.

In the "Moment of Truth" he finds the purity of his own spirit—and we find ourselves being sold insurance by the St. Paul Insurance Company.

Using the setting of a bullfighter in the arena, the St. Paul Insurance Company tells us in a television commercial we have to prepare for unexpected risks in life—"...like, say, the bull coming from behind," as the commercial says in part.

One reason resonance of the Hispanic world has become so attenuated is that it increasingly serves more precise commercial aims, and companies paying for the resonance want just that, and nothing more.

Just as the more linguistically textual version of SalsaSpeak, this Hispanic imagery has its own inner consistency and logic.

And it's been a boon for pop culture's creative people, enabling them to pack in as much Hispanic Resonance as possible into advertising, movies, television dramas and comedies, public service announcements and even television news coverage and "promos."

An ABC Television "promo" (airing Aug. 26, 2000) for an upcoming golf tournament on the network two days later matching Sergio Garcia (a Spaniard) against the more famous American golfer "Tiger" Woods, showed Garcia dressed as a matador. And, through the magic of television technology and special effects, Garcia was waving his matador cape in front of a real tiger, representing, obviously, "Tiger" Woods.

The ease—and now predictability—with which popular culture converts Hispanic culture into familiar images for mass audiences must inevitably have some sort of mind-numbing (if not actually mind-rotting) effect on people. When the real complexity of an entire culture—or even a particular Hispanic country's culture (in this case, Spain, which in pop culture's visual vocabulary is what this presentation of bullfighting generally signifies)—can be distilled into the intricacy of the designs of the matador's "suit of lights," then perception and thought must certainly suffer.

Perhaps if the bullfighting image was more regularly offered as a promotional "hook" for documentaries on Spain or other programming actually about Hispanics, it wouldn't be as bad. But we are talking here—in this example—about a *golf tournament*, unlikely to be productive of much real knowledge about Hispanics and Hispanic culture.

The higher Hispanic harmonies of Hispanic Resonance come in convenient consumer "portions," whatever one's taste and intellectual inclination.

This is something Americans of all ages can share in.

Take the great Spanish artist Pablo Picasso, for example. This is just what a 1998 movie entitled "Big and Hairy," has done. The movie's title is not intended as a physical description of Pablo Picasso. But this (by now) legendary Spanish artist does figure prominently, metaphorically, in the movie, whose young protagonist is named "Picasso." Well, that's his first name.

"Picasso" here is a young middle-school student, who with the aid of a "Bigfoot" beast (the title "character") eventually helps his basketball team win the championship.

The intriguing thing is how the screenwriter has simply popped this appellative angle into a setting and plotline that has absolutely nothing (other than this echoing resonance of the famous Spanish painter) to do with Hispanics. And yet, somehow, it doesn't seem out of place at all. In fact, as the screenwriter must have surmised would happen, it gives the young boy a greater charm and coloring (as a character) than he might otherwise have. He is, after all, in every other respect, just an average kid. And that's part of his problem fitting in, since his less-than-polished basketball skills help him to lose an important game for his team. But when he is called by his name—by his parents, for example—the simple fact of his first name, *Picasso*, imbues him with more personality, makes him an inspiring figure.

Picasso. This is someone—albeit a middle-school basketball player in a small town struggling to fit into new surroundings and with new people—who can do great things. And he does, bringing the new best friend he has made—the "Bigfoot" beast—onto the team and winning, in the final seconds, the championship game of the season.

In a fanciful movie like this, a movie admittedly aimed to younger viewers and not concerned with great social issues like the integration of Hispanics into the mainstream of American society, there does seem to be some significant "mainstreaming" going on here. It is, of course, the seamless and seemingly effortless "integration" of "salsafied" Hispanic Resonance into American pop culture and life.

And it shows how even the high end of Hispanic Resonance—the "upscale" part of Hispanic life and culture represented by an artistic genius like Picasso—can be trimmed to fit into something as light and airy as an affectionate satire (it seems) of adolescent coming-of-age movies.

This is an American popular culture determined to make of Hispanic life and culture—as someone once described the mission of German philosophers approaching the field of aesthetics—conquered territory, to bring every possible resonance of it, for every possible purpose and situation, into play as needed.

The masterful achievement of this task is on dazzling display in American pop culture and more "public," serious life, a palpable presence in American movies, television, advertising, and increasingly in politics and the Hispanic-flavored speech and writing with which journalists and just everyday people interpret life and express themselves.

It is perhaps a mark of this pervading presence, of its obvious and often preening success, that it no longer seems notable (apparently) to average Americans who live in places in America where there are few if any Hispanics and yet who see this Hispanic Resonance as an integral part of the pop culture (and more serious fashioning of American life) by which they are surrounded.

In effect, Hispanics—in a very real and vital way—have been "accepted" by average Americans. Of course, it's not Hispanics as individual, complex people who have been accepted. It's the "salsafied" view of Hispanics—the pop culture view now being extended and applied to American political and "public" life—that has been accepted as a plausible idea of who Hispanics are and what they offer to other, non-Hispanic Americans.

Or maybe, more precisely, Hispanics—the idea of them as these "salsafied" people who offer up their enlivening spirit in service to America—have now been *absorbed* into average Americans' lives.

And Picasso may be a superlative example of this process, unfolding, to be sure, over decades but (as in the movie "Big and Hairy") proving to be capable (in pop culture's hands) of being ever more effectively molded and "morph"-able.

For reducing Picasso to the simplistic level at which pop culture applications can be deftly made is a remarkable achievement when one considers how art critics and historians have a difficult time cogently encapsulating his achievements and body of work.

To appreciate, therefore, the magnitude of pop culture's triumph in *processing* Picasso for less lofty applications than his multi-dimensional life and work might seem to merit or warrant, we must take a deeper look at just what Americans are *absorbing* about Hispanics, and how this process works.

The convergence of Hispanic knowledge, or *information* that can be applied to new needs, and the absorption of this information on a massive scale (which is what pop culture helps to accomplish) are the issues at hand.

When people feel the elasticity of such knowledge as a tangible thing—as pop culture uses of Picasso can show over time—it must seem only natural to absorb this sense of it as actual knowledge, as if one actually does know something important about Picasso, or Hispanics.

What's equally (at least) as interesting is how other aspects, non-Hispanic ones, of pop culture-produced "knowledge" can be brought to bear to "understand" Hispanics like, in this case, Picasso.

When allied with other pop culture-produced "insights" to help build the framework of basic knowledge about Hispanics, the process of absorption is not only accelerated but also authenticated in substantial ways (substantial, that is, from the point of view of American "information consumers").

If something about Hispanics fits in with what people know, or think they know, about how life works, then it becomes easier to assimilate and absorb such information.

This can work in the other direction as well. Knowledge about Hispanics already processed into the popular consciousness can become a means, as is ever more frequently shown, to understand new, non-Hispanic-connected, information.

Picasso is a prominent example of this as well.

To understand how big Jackie Gleason is in the food business in New Jersey in the 1960's movie "Don't Drink The Water," a character in the film describes him as the "Potato Salad Picasso."

If a collective sigh of "ahhh" did not emanate from audiences seeing the movie for the first time and thereby (by such a description) fully comprehending the Gleason character's talent and success in his food marketing enterprise, this example still amply illustrates the process at work.

Sometimes, of course, over the decades of American popular culture, the mention of Picasso *does* have something to do with Picasso.

In the 1960 movie "The Apartment," a Picasso reference adds an ironic touch to the movie. And it was not apparently a hindrance to the critical success of the movie, which won "Oscars" for best picture and best original screenplay.

In the "Picasso scene," a character has a quizzical reaction to a painting by Picasso.

Picasso, in fact, seems to be one of the signal ways in which a character or situation in a movie or other pop culture entertainment gets to be explained to us. And exemplifying the ease with which pop culture pops in Hispanic resonance, Picasso references appear in all kinds of non-Hispanic contexts as a way to make comprehensible the character or point being portrayed or offered.

The clear meaning of the Picasso scene in "The Apartment"—adding to the urbane and quirky sophistication of the film—is that Picasso is odd.

Well, maybe not Picasso the man—the film does not deal with the biography of Picasso—but certainly Picasso the artist. He may be great, but he's strange—his work is strange and this is information, knowledge, offered about Picasso.

When such direct offerings about Picasso are linked together over time they become part of the continuum of "knowledge" about Hispanics given to average, non-Hispanic Americans.

An A&E cable channel "Biography Special" on Picasso several years ago may be an example of the intensifying presentation of pop culture "reports" about Picasso.

And such an extended provision of "knowledge" about one of the most important Hispanics to have ever lived and one of the seminal figures in world art is an opportunity to bring together the strands (many of them, certainly) of pop culture's ideas about Picasso and, by extension, the "salsafied" Hispanic world.

The frame of reference—the mediating means of teaching us about Picasso on a level and in a way we can comprehend it without necessarily knowing anything about art or Picasso's stylistic roots, before coming to the program—is Picasso the highly emotional artist.

Everyone *knows* about emotions, everyone (probably) *has* emotions.

And so Picasso—as presented on the A&E program—is "accessible" to everyone, and not just people who have taken the time and effort to learn about Picasso the artist, and the incredible journey of artistic imagination and creation *for decades* that was also his life.

If the argument is here raised that the very many people—the vast majority of ordinary Americans, it might be safe to say—who are not planning to invest the time and effort to substantively study Picasso should be given the opportunity to appreciate him, as with an A&E "Biography Special," it must be answered in a larger context. Namely, with blurring distinctions—the Hispanic Resonance replacing reasoned knowledge—brought on by pop culture.

Offering up the idea—as the A&E program clearly does—that one receives an insight into Picasso's art by an approach to the man based on emotion, that one can thereby "understand" his work in a way not otherwise possible, without much reference or appeal to artistic tradition and styles, is disturbing.

And although we are primarily concerned here with the impact of trivializing Hispanic artistic greatness as just one more aspect of pop culture's view of "salsafied," spirited Hispanic life and culture, the danger of such trivialization hurts non-Hispanic Americans as well, as has already been suggested.

It encourages a cast of mind, a way of thinking (and non-thinking), a self-deception that one has accomplished some feat of knowledge acquisition without what have heretofore been considered requisite means of acquiring knowledge.

The exercise of one's mental faculties to learn something significant about a seminal Latino artist like Picasso would itself be an actual demonstration (to the non-Hispanic who undertakes it) of the complexity of Hispanic people and culture.

Conversely, being able to attain to an understanding of the highest Hispanic artistic achievements—based on pop culture-provided information—without having to stretch one's mind is a living example as well. Proving, it seems, that Hispanic culture is simplistic at its center, understandable to everyone who can appreciate its essential emotion.

Of course, one of the best arguments that can be made for the continued practice of Hispanic Resonance is that it works so well for so many things.

Be the purpose serious or satiric, in the venue of popular culture or political culture, a "positive" or "negative" view of Hispanics, Hispanic Resonance is eminently adaptable.

A similar example (to the A&E "Biography Special") comes in the 1997 movie "Incognito," which shows how the quality of knowledge about Picasso (and Hispanics) being absorbed into the American consciousness is a specious one.

This is again the nuanced connection made between emotion and knowledge, helping to replace reason and the "products" of reason, like (in the case of art) knowledge of the principles of art, and the particular "tradition" in which an artist worked (or helped to create, as in the actual story of Picasso).

Emotion can be a form of knowledge, as valid in its way as the forms of knowledge represented by reason, the movie suggests.

This is supremely the case, of course, for *knowledge* about Hispanics, who in the view of pop culture's "salsafied" model are practically pure, distilled emotion or spicy "spirit."

The appropriate cast of mind aids this intuition of Hispanic harmonies—of the highest Hispanic harmonies.

Passion is good, perhaps even indispensable.

In "Incognito," Jason Patric is a young American artist who's driven by his obsession with great art, living in Europe in the art world of auctions, sophistication, museums, and, most of all, *intrigue*...

Patric gets caught up with art forgers, but his basic goodness is validated by his intensity of emotion about Picasso and great art. His intensity here takes the place of what is often referred to as aesthetic contemplation. This aesthetic appreciation of the work of a great painter like Picasso can be emotional as well (at least in part), but it is traditionally informed by actual knowledge of principles of art composition, history of art, and the style (or styles) of the artist.

The aesthetic contemplation is thus a fusion of real, substantive knowledge and the very real (emotional) excitement about seeing a masterpiece (or multiple ones) in which the artist has realized high aesthetic harmonies.

Ultimately, no matter how dramatically presented or urgently pressed, resonance about great artists like Picasso cannot replace reasoned (and informed) knowledge, which in the moment of aesthetic contemplation is, or should be, a purer, more rarefied emotion anyway.

The absurdity here noted is only one of the many presented by pop culture's "salsafied," distorted view of Hispanic life and culture.

But it is one fraught with many dangers for the mind of average non-Hispanic Americans (and eventually for Hispanics too), as we have already alluded to.

What must jump out as one of the dangers, without having to offer elaborate explanations, is the foreclosing of the need to actually learn something substantial about art and artists before feeling one can proclaim their greatness. This seems especially disturbing when one realizes how—confronted with the fact of so many competing ideas of Hispanics that are negative or trivialized—a genuine study of Picasso could be one way of presenting a positive view of Hispanics to non-Hispanics.

This seems, at root, the only possible way to really counter stereotypes about Hispanics. With, that is, an in-depth encounter based on real knowledge of Hispanic culture and history, such as one leading to a true aesthetic appreciation of Picasso. Hyped appeals about greatness and how we should feel such an intense emotional sense of Picasso's genius—even if successful—are simply superficial and only do damage to any widespread view of Hispanics.

But they help give non-Hispanics the methods and "materials" from which to be "programmers" of their own Hispanic Resonance, "Conquistadors," in effect, of the "world" of Hispanic Resonance.

This is a feeling which can stand one, as a non-Hispanic, in good stead in the quest to become a Fiesta Person—a "surrogate" Hispanic, as it were—built on the actual sensory experience of the Hispanic fiesta elements of food (and drink), music, dance, and design.

It is this "Sensory Search"—and this quest—to which we will now turn.

CHAPTER 3

THE SENSORY SEARCH

"He brings this 'Hot Tamale' up to his room…"
—Richard Belzer in the 1996 movie "Not of This Earth."

No one has gone as berserk over "Salsafication" as a pair of white women who call themselves "The Too Hot Tamales."

They write cookbooks, run restaurants, and make personal appearances.

But most of all, they *personify* spicy Hispanic spirit, *fiesta* spirit.

And they do something else as well.

They offer *hope*.

Hope to ordinary white people everywhere of a better life, a *spicier* life.

Their real names, their actual names, are Mary Sue Milliken and Susan Feniger.

But their self-anointment as *personas* proselytizing the mystique and meaning of Hispanic spirit to non-Hispanics is their real identity…

Hey, we're the "Too Hot Tamales," and we're as spicy as our Mexican food! And we want to help you become "Hot Tamales" too!

In the new America, the America being remade in the spirit of "salsafication," "The Too Hot Tamales" take on a supreme importance as groundbreakers, pathfinders, *pioneers*.

They are white and yet, by the possibilities invested in them (and other non-Hispanic Americans) as Americans capable of commanding their own destinies—deciding on whomever (and for whatever length of time) they want to be—they have become "surrogate" Hispanics.

"The Too Hot Tamales" have undertaken no standardized course of study, undergone no special transformation other than that dictated by their own desire.

And their *plausibility* as presenters of not only Hispanic cultural elements but also Hispanic personality itself is unquestioned, if their success is any measure.

With their Mexican cookbooks and Mexican restaurants and personal appearances to demonstrate Mexican food cooking techniques, the duo is nothing so much as a personal conglomerate built on the Hispanic fiesta and elements.

For people fortunate enough to live near one of the pair's restaurants—"The Border Grill" in Los Angeles, for example—there is the particular delight of partaking of the fiesta spirit directly (almost) from them.

The "...Tamales" will not only deliver Mexican food to your home (well, not the "...Tamales" *themselves*, but their *representatives* certainly), they will deliver a *fiesta*, complete with mariachis (assuming one has made the proper arrangements and paid the appropriate fees).

The Production of **Authenticity**

In the peculiar logic at work in America, there is a special—even ecstatic, it appears—delight in receiving fiesta elements and spirit from the "...Tamales'" eatery, for the "...Tamales" have authentically mediated the "chain of custody" of the fiesta from its roots residing with Hispanic people.

Even if the "...Tamales" have not received some sort of official stamp of approval from a Hispanic Academy granting "surrogate" Hispanichood, they have indeed journeyed to Mexican locations to discover and document their cookbook recipes and restaurant dishes.

And thus the duo presents *authenticity*, which is certainly helped in these home-delivered *fiestas* with the presence of the mariachis.

The "...Tamales" rocketed to fame with their (former) show on the "Food Network" cable channel.

It helped them to build audiences for their books and restaurants and personal cooking demonstrations.

But their significance in this book is not founded on the specifics of their success, although this success forms the basis for their *exemplar* as *meaning*, but on what it tells us about the nascent *Fiesta Nation* of America, in its ascendancy.

For it is, essentially, a success story in the best American tradition, a stock *Storyline* in the larger American *Story*.

A pair of inventive, dedicated, and (to be sure) hard-working Americans come up with an idea for a product to improve the lives of other, average Americans.

Their invention—Themselves.

But—as the old saying goes about timing being everything—they found just the right moment in the unfolding Story of America to launch themselves as "The Too Hot Tamales," to *become* part of America's *Story*.

In the "Long Goodbye" to Hispanic people—the development over decades in American popular culture of a "Hispanic Resonance" able to be manipulated for non-Hispanic meaning and purposes—the "...Tamales" were able to divine that the time was right to take Hispanic Resonance to an all-new level.

Become the Resonance. *Become* "surrogate" Hispanics.

Of all the items available for purchase at the duo's restaurants, or available in their cookbooks for duplication in one's kitchen, there is nothing so delicious as their "invention" of themselves.

Joyously zany, "The Too Hot Tamales" suggest how America's *Story* is evolving, enriching itself from Hispanic Resonance—a Hispanic Resonance that can be enjoyed, that can be *personified*, without Hispanic people being directly involved.

Most of the time, anyway, because there are those Mexican mariachis ready to be dispatched to one's own home, in the environs of "The Border Grill," for one's further enjoyment of the home-delivered "Fiesta" meal.

Of course, in sheer numbers, the number of people who enjoy this kind of "fiesta" from the "...Tamales" is likely less than the number of Americans who have seen the "...Tamales" on television (on their former "Food Network" program), bought their cookbooks or seen them at a personal appearance.

Their "lesson" to white (and other non-Hispanic) Americans is the "lesson" of the *Sensory Search*, the subject we are exploring in this chapter.

It is that non-Hispanic Americans can become "surrogate" Hispanics (to the depth and degree of their desire) by the sensory sensations of Hispanic fiesta elements and the emotional resonance evoked by these sensations.

This "personification" of the great irony, the absurdity on a massive scale, of "celebrating" Hispanic spirit on the basis of the fiesta element, *Mexican food*, often used to belittle and even excoriate Hispanics, is part of the "...Tamales'" saucy appeal.

No one—as far as we know—points this out about "The Too Hot Tamales" in the popular media. It is the supremely "Private Joke" of the "...Tamales."

But it is inescapable. And in our examination of it, of the troubling questions it raises abut the larger "salsafication" of America—as well as the impact it has on individual white (and other non-Hispanic) Americans' pursuit of the "Sensory Search" of Hispanic sensation and spirit—we will find it critical to our understanding of the "...Tamales'" importance as social phenomenon.

In this examination of the "...Tamales'" as *personal demonstration* of "The Private Joke" we enter (or enter more deeply) an "Alice-in-Wonderland" kind of world.

The wondrous new world of Hispanic culture—that opens to one in pop culture's celebration of Hispanic sensory sensations and its promotion of "salsafied" Hispanic products—can be seen as something valuable for non-Hispanics when, for the same reasons, it has been viewed as something horrible about Hispanics.

It is celebrated now—now that it involves white (and other non-Hispanic) Americans in "salsafication" from Hispanic spirit and elements—for the same reasons it was heretofore scorned when it only (or primarily) involved Hispanics.

In terms of food, the same food that helped to fuel the stereotypes of Hispanics as slothful, greasy, and spicy (the "You-Are-What-You-Eat" argument, and if the food you eat is spicy, well...) is now praised for the same qualities it has as food, with the same traditions and cooking techniques that it had before. With regard to the "You-Are-What-You-Eat" idea, "The Too Hot Tamales" may have become spicy people, at least in theory, because they have had so much spicy Mexican food. And that's a *good* thing—for them. They have built a career on this *persona*, on being spicy, just like their Mexican food. On the same basis, that is, as Hispanics have been caricatured (in a grimly negative way, for of course the "Too Hot Tamales" are a "positive" caricature created by the "...Tamales" themselves) and castigated as less than admirable people. The "Alice-in-Wonderland" tone of all this is even more pronounced when one realizes that Hispanic food is still available for use as unregenerate racism (and comic relief in pop culture) against Hispanics.

Overlooking this history (and current practice) is kind of like saying, *Don't really need to think about that, don't really mean anything by it, it's not really related to what's happening now...*

Of course, for people who *were* called, say, "chili chokers" in their lifetimes (simply because of their Latin ethnicity), and who must today watch some of the nation's best-known and most-visible comedians use the same food-based humor against Hispanics that is, apparently, perfectly comprehensible and plausible (and funny!) to non-Hispanics who certainly must be eating some of the same Hispanic food, it's unlikely *they* can overlook it.

To gloss over all this, to nominally overlook it at the same time it is part of the "...Tamales'" deliberate resonance, is part of the profound disrespect for Hispanic people symbolized by America's "salsafication" and by the "Sensory Search."

For the very idea—essential to the *meaning* of the "Sensory Search" for non-Hispanics intent on their "salsafication" from Hispanic spirit and sensation—of Hispanic people as so easily *reproducible* by means of their food and drink, music, dance and design is spectacularly disrespectful and demeaning. And what is more worrisome yet is the idea about how the "...Tamales'" success suggests how, in a bizarre but highly plausible way, non-Hispanic Americans may feel they make *better* Hispanics than actual Hispanics.

The little history of prejudice based on food we have offered here can make this plain.

Non-Hispanics who think about it at all, who understand the "Private Joke" of "The Too Hot Tamales," also immediately realize they don't carry this "historical" or social "baggage."

They can engage in the exuberant pursuit of Mexican food and other Hispanic elements of the "Sensory Search" without any fear of suffering discrimination based on it.

In fact, they may even be "celebrated" for it.

These are the now-famous "Chili-Heads," for instance, principally white Americans (it appears), who are praised for their passionate devotion to Chile Peppers and their myriad applications in Mexican (and other) foods.

And while "Chili-Heads" don't want to literally be "Chili-Chokers" (they don't want to *choke* on Chile peppers), they do want other people to discover the "world" of spicy sensation they have now discovered.

And in this *crusade*, the "Chili-Heads" have science on their side.

Or more precisely, the science of physiology.

In the January 1996 issue of the "Discovery Channel Magazine," a little article details why spicy Mexican food may be so "addicting."

"Anyone who has accidentally bitten into a hot chili pepper knows it can cause an explosion in the mouth comparable to an earthquake...with all the burn chili peppers produce, it's surprising that so many people are drawn to them. But studies have shown that the brain secretes a natural painkiller in response to the heat that triggers a pleasurable feeling for the chili-eater, and even causes some people to get heated. For chili pepper junkies, and for those who come in close contact with them, that's an addiction that gives the term 'dragon breath' a new dimension."

This helps to explain the physiology behind the current, non-Hispanic craze for hot Mexican food, and easy, nonchalant way that a regular dietary engagement with Chile Peppers can evolve from a racist rant (Hispanics as "chili chokers" in one of the standard phrases from a prejudiced past) to an appreciation of "Chile Pepper junkies" or "Chili-Heads."

This January 1996 issue of "Discovery Channel Magazine" also makes other, for our purposes, salient points.

Including the idea about how easily Hispanic people are *replaced* by their food.

The difference between food and (Hispanic) people is deftly bridged, and they are metaphorically melded, interchangeably considered.

The magazine's brief article about Chile peppers is headlined "Fiery Temperament."

Temperament. You know, *what people have.* A temperament, a personality.

And in the same issue of "Discovery Channel Magazine," support is offered for would-be (or active) "Chili-Heads" with information on pertinent programming. The program listings include an entry for the series "The Burger Meister With Marcel DeSaulniers" for Jan. 13, 1996. On this episode, "The Burger Meister" showed one "how to prepare a flank steak chiliburger and black bean chili."

"Chili-Heads" are also vital to our exploration of "The Sensory Search."

For their cultish fascination with *authenticity*, with Chile Pepper varieties and cultivation and "chain of custody" from suppliers and particular points of origin, sets forth one of the main principles of the "Sensory Search," namely, the idea of best becoming a "surrogate" Hispanic by most closely replicating the sensory sensations of Hispanic people enjoying their cultural elements like food.

And with this in mind, authenticity, or the *appearance* of it, becomes all-important.

We've touched on this point with "The Too Hot Tamales," whose books detail their efforts to carefully gather and develop their recipes from the original, authentic sources—Hispanic people.

In this lesson for would-be *aficionados*—white people who want to taste the *authenticity* and feel the spicy resonance of Hispanic culture when they eat Mexican food and enjoy the other tangible Hispanic elements—"The Too Hot Tamales" and the "Chili-Heads" embarked on the tutelage of American tastes and temperaments have plenty of company, like corporations working to "personalize" the Hispanic fiesta experience for non-Hispanics.

As with SalsaSpeak—the use of Spanish-language and Hispanic elements to "spice up" American speech and writing—the *meaning* of the Sensory Search has also become widely comprehensible to non-Hispanic Americans.

The shorthand use of this meaning, the easy exegesis of this explanation in summary fashion as time goes on, is striking. It's clear from commercials, from the little lexicon or subset of SalsaSpeak used in them, how transformational the sensory experience—allied with those emotional evocations of Hispanic spirit—of Hispanic elements like food (and drink) can be.

In most cases, of course, these transformations—these ventures into "surrogate" Hispanichood—are temporary, about as long, perhaps, as it takes to visit a "Chi Chi's" or other chain Mexican restaurant for lunch or dinner.

That's perfectly okay, apparently.

"Chi Chi's" and the Mexican Food "Revolution"

"Chi Chi's" and other chain Mexican restaurant operations—indeed the wide array of "salsafied" Hispanic-style products and the companies advertising them—have taken this reality into account.

We are, after all, not yet at a point in this chapter where we will examine "The Fiesta Lifestyle," as exemplified by actual *big* places (entire cities or portions, thereof, like San Antonio, Texas) and the more determinedly, and prolonged, transformation into *Hispanicity* for non-Hispanics.

Before we go there, *before we get there*, we must examine how *place* delineated by the building and interior of, say, a "Chi Chi's" chain Mexican restaurant serves America's "salsafication" of non-Hispanics.

"Chi Chi's" takes advantage of the *place in the mind*, a *place* where happy Hispanics are perpetually at play in a happy fiesta.

For the imaginatively deficient, however, "Chi Chi's" is still prepared.

The idea of "place" as providing "salsafication"—joined to the food offering "salsafication"—must not be overlooked. The "integration" of fiesta elements—including food and design—neatly substitutes for (and neatly summarizes) the "authentic" and idealized Hispanic place where an actual fiesta would be taking place. This saves a trip to the Hispanic "barrio" (if one is nearby to begin with) to search for such a "fiesta" and its ambient "place."

It is, in fact, a full-service "salsafier," beginning with SalsaSpeak.

Starting with its slogan—"Life Always Needs A Little Salsa"—"Chi Chi's" presents a *philosophy*, further detailed in its "Declaration of Salsafication," which comes under the branch of philosophy known as Hedonism, *Hispanic Division.*

The full "Declaration" is as follows…

"When in the course of human events, it becomes necessary to solemnly declare the right to be free and salsafied: absolved from all connection to the shackles of the bored, the ordinary and the bland.

"We hold these truths to be self-evident, that all Chi Chi's are created to salsafy our lives through good food, festive drink and the pursuit of some serious fun.

"Further, it is the right of the people to abolish routine. As a free and salsafied people, you have the full power to come together, to eat, to drink, to laugh, to be loud, to relax, to goof off, to pause.

"On support of this declaration, we pledge to you these articles of salsafication for as long as the sun does rise.

For...Life always needs a little Salsa."

This is, in effect, a declaration of sovereignty for a Hispanic realm of the imagination—a world of sensation and spirit—the entrance into which we are afforded by a visit to "Chi Chi's."

Indeed, "Chi Chi's" is dealing as much (or more) in the business of applied Hispanic Resonance as it is in Mexican-style food and drink.

"Chi Chi's" sees "salsafication" everywhere. The slogans are impressive enough—cleverly characterizing pop culture's spirit—but what may be most intriguing about this worldview is the chain's idea about its impact on communities. The company sends out press releases with titles like "Chi-Chi's Re-Salsafies The Plaza in New Jersey" (release of May 24, 1999), which details how "America's Favorite Mexican Restaurant chain...is celebrating the grand re-opening of its Seacaucus restaurant located in the Harmon Meadows Plaza shopping mall." The picture that unavoidably jumps to mind is "Urban Renewal *Plus*." A raising of the *spirit* of the place in which the restaurant is located, an enlivened environment where people are made happier and feel better about their lot and lives. Whether this is exactly what "Chi Chi's" has in mind is unclear, but it certainly has *something* in mind with the tenor and wording of its releases.

A more apt adage for the company might be...*Salsafy* everything in sight!

Obviously, the "salsafication" going on *inside* the restaurant (for paying customers) is thus no less monumental than the one going on *outside*.

Where does this stop? Perhaps as *Public Policy*.

A Big-city Mayor bursts into a meeting of his city planners, slams a thick folder (filled with "Chi Chi's" press releases) down on the table, and says "I want this city *salsafied* now!"

At this rate, "Chi Chi's" may single-handedly solve the problem of how to revitalize America's "inner cities"—*Salsafy* them!

Put "Chi Chi's" Mexican restaurants—with their "contemporary design elements" and "salsa attitude" as the aforementioned press release specifies—into critical areas of crumbling or abandoned urban areas and you'll bring them back to life *pronto*, sprucing up those neighborhoods and sparking a renewal of the spirit among the residents and business owners. Based on the language of "Chi Chi's" publicity mill, these things seem like real possibilities.

The chain also adheres to the idea of using the word "fiesta" as often as possible, fiesta being somewhat interchangeable with salsa (salsa in its broader sense of signifying spiciness in life) and in related terms (the salsa spirit being basically the fiesta spirit or the essence of the fiesta). Among recent "fiesta" line products from "Chi Chi's" are "Fiesta Salsa" and "Fiesta For Four" take-out meals. These items suggest the depth of this commitment to remain consistent about the company's promotions of not only the products but also the idea and spirit informing them. And it is in keeping with pop culture practice to plainly state its fiesta concept, in case people aren't paying attention, or because they might mistake the fun or enjoyment they are having for just any old fun rather than the ratcheted-up fun of the fiesta—spicier and more spirited even when it is only invoked in name and doesn't actually involve any features of a traditional fiesta.

"Chi Chi's" and other chain Mexican restaurants are, in effect, "Salsafication stations," never letting up on the coordinated campaign to build newer, non-Hispanic, Fiesta People.

"Chi Chi's," of course, makes this as explicit as possible with its "Declaration of Salsafication."

The restaurant aims at creating a complete "salsafication experience," in an imaginative a way as possible.

And with its "home-replacement" meals—not really a food-delivery service, since one needs to actually pick up the prepared entrees from the restaurant itself—"Chi Chi's" takes its Resonance applications into people's homes.

That's the theory, anyway, as "Chi Chi's" makes clear—in its press releases and on its website.

Even if people aren't exactly sure what to feel when eating a "home-replacement fiesta meal" inside one's abode, "Chi Chi's" has some suggestions.

"As the nation's leader in full service, casual dining Mexican restaurants, we are famous for great-tasting, traditional Mexican cuisine combined with a fun, festive dining experience. Now you can take this experience home with you."

In recent years, "Chi Chi's" has shown a series of commercials on television in which a young white American has journeyed to Mexico to find new dishes for the restaurant to serve back home (in the United States).

Well, maybe. In point of fact, "Chi Chi's" test kitchens are located in Kentucky.

That's not a bit of information widely shared with the American public, and the reason is patently obvious.

It would hurt the campaign, the *blitzkrieg*, really, of precisely applied Hispanic Resonance "Chi Chi's" is waging.

"Chi Chi's" may actually be the most efficient "corporate raider" of Hispanic Resonance—for the purpose of "salsafying" non-Hispanic Americans—as there is in America today.

The use of this Hispanic Resonance for "salsafication" does not lift Hispanic-Americans, does not do anything for them, even if it *appears* to do so. And it is critical to keep this in mind as we explore the ramifications of "The Sensory Search."

Building the necessity of Hispanic people into the philosophical framework of "The Sensory Search"—*you have to be served a "Margarita" drink by a "Hispanic" for the drink's magic evocation of the Hispanic world to work*, for example—would simply be an inefficiency.

Consider just one complication.

The decisions on where to locate chain Mexican restaurants were not based on the demographics of Hispanic population and its growth.

And thus, the uniformity of a Hispanic workforce in chain Mexican restaurants was never a consideration, since many of these chain operations are in places with few Hispanic residents. For this reason—maybe especially for this reason—the idea of the *standardization* of proffered Hispanic spirit in all of the chains' restaurants is the goal.

To this end, the chain restaurants' design elements are intended to help non-Hispanic Americans imaginatively project themselves into the harmonies of Hispanic experience symbolized by the fiesta.

For *celebrating* Hispanics, *celebrating* their sensation and spirit—and bringing (as an evangelist might say) the "good news" of Hispanic culture to non-Hispanics is what "salsafication" is all about.

Mmmm, this is really good Mexican food, really authentic...you know, I'm beginning to feel a little Hispanic...

Add the décor, the *surroundings* including the *sound design* of the Latin music in the background and it is quite possible to believe (especially if one wants to) that one is indeed in a self-contained little sanctuary of Hispanic Resonance.

A sanctuary connected directly to the Hispanic world of spicy spirit and elements, like, thankfully, food, for which one can feel particularly grateful to "Chi Chi's." And even if a "Chi Chi's" restaurant is a *forward outpost*, far from Mexico or the Southwestern United States—where the Hispanic Resonance is a natural part of history and heritage—it is nonetheless a place of Hispanic-resonant refuge.

"Chi Chi's" is one of the "leaders" of the Mexican food "revolution" in America, along with "El Torito" and "Taco Bell," spearheading the "intellectual" underpinnings of this revolution.

Broadly stated (and including what pop culture more generally is doing to promote its Hispanic-style products), this "revolution" seeks to "salsafy" American tastes for obvious commercial purposes.

"Salsafication" is, by now, so established in American popular culture that "re-salsafication" can take place, as the previously-noted "Chi-Chi's" press release makes clear.

"Re-salsafication"—the "second-generation" re-tooling and refinement of "salsafication" to better conform to Americans' desires and tastes for a more complete fiesta "experience."

In another typical press release—this one dated Aug. 29, 2000 and entitled "Chi-Chi's Is Re-Salsafied in Clarksville, Indiana"—the chain restaurant offers its *definition* of "Re-Salsafication."

"The remodeled restaurant features a brand new décor package reflecting Chi-Chi's new 'salsa attitude' with a contemporary design which is lighter and brighter creating a more casual atmosphere. The design elements enhance the overall visual appeal of the restaurant."

The release goes on to explain its commitment to what might be described as an ongoing evolutionary process.

"We have been in this community for the past 16 years and have enjoyed serving the people of Clarksville and the surrounding areas. We are proud to provide our guests with yet another exciting dimension to their dining experience at Chi-Chi's. The new menu we introduced a couple of months ago, combined with our tradition of salsa-rific service—and now this new, festive and colorful dining environment collectively creates a dining experience that is both fun and unique."

In one of "Chi Chi's" more recent campaigns, it proclaims a trip to one of its restaurants is like "visiting a little bit of Mexico."

And "Chi Chi's" targets this promotion to *teachers*, who are urged to bring in their students for a videotape about Mexico, "special gifts" representing Mexico, and, of course, a luncheon meal emblematic of a meal in Mexico.

"Chi Chi's" restaurants—Educators Extraordinaire. But why stop there? How about diplomatic initiatives bringing together the countries of Mexico and the United States? How does the Mexican Embassy feel? Can they—the Mexican officials from the Embassy and those in the Foreign Relations offices of the Mexican Government in Mexico City—endorse the effort?

The "Chi Chi's" educational initiatives—on the tour for students—thus range from history and geography to folk arts ("See the sombrero on the wall, kids, well that signifies...") and finally, inevitably, the "cuisine" of the country of Mexico. (The "cuisine" perfected, as we have already said, in the "test kitchens" in Kentucky.)

This is such a shameless endeavor that it can't help but raise even more ridiculous speculations.

Is "Chi Chi's" planning to coordinate with other relevant bodies and organizations? Will it cooperate, in some fashion, with the country's Hispanic Studies and Chicano Studies programs in colleges and universities?

The symbolic significance of this is staggering. "Chi Chi's" is speaking *on behalf of Mexico*, doing what Mexico would do if it had the resources to directly sponsor education and public relations outreach to Americans at dozens of places in the United States.

With "Chi Chi's" educating people about Mexico, one wonders what is to be gained or given to non-Hispanic Americans for the *extra* effort of actually visiting Mexico. Once you've been to a "Chi Chi's" or "El Torito" or other chain Mexican restaurant, what more do you need, in terms of your Mexico *experience*? Well, maybe a visit to "Mexico" at Disney World in Florida, which offers the "country" of Mexico in its International Pavilion.

"Processing" Hispanic People Into "Fiesta Spirit"

In this new world of "salsafied" commerce—relying on and resonating a fiesta-flavored Hispanic "world"—Hispanics as people are rendered irrelevant as they are rendered (in food processing terms) into their essence of spirit.

Our earlier statement about the irrelevance of Hispanics as employees does not mean chain operations are unmindful of the role their employees play in creating and maintaining the happy Hispanic daydream underway.

Just as revolutionary is what "El Torito" chain Mexican restaurants—formerly owned by the same parent company that owns "Chi Chi's"—are doing. "El Torito" is offering the authenticity of Hispanic spirit and warmth, it says, despite reality, logic, common sense, and the individuality of the people hired by "El Torito" to work in its restaurants.

What kind of training program does the restaurant have to enable its people, including non-Hispanics, to offer such authentic Hispanic spirit? And, at the end of a particularly pleasant meal, does a family compliment a white waiter by saying something to the effect that...*now we know what authentic Hispanic warmth and spirit is like*. There seems to be no self-doubt about "El Torito's" belief in its ability to pull this one off. It is a corporate commitment. *We will do this*.

The "El Torito" Mexican restaurant chain has "processed" the Hispanic spirit—specifically the Mexican spirit—and offers it up as part of the "menu," more broadly speaking, to be enjoyed on a visit to the restaurant.

It is not an unproductive exercise to wonder how "El Torito" has achieved this, what advances in training technology it has discovered and implemented in its preparation of wait staff before they are ever deemed ready to meet the public.

"El Torito" could help solve the "service with a smile" crisis in America.

The growth of the service industry—including the boom in fast food restaurants of all kinds—in America has not been equaled by a similar spurt in the numbers of happy, friendly people available to work in its ranks.

And if there are not enough Hispanics ("The Fiesta People") to go around in all the places they would be needed in America, then the next best thing would certainly be the conversion of non-Hispanics into hospitable, *Hispanic-like*, people.

The chain makes this idea about presenting authentic Hispanic hospitality plain in its press releases, *so people will know*.

On the occasion of "breaking ground" for its 100th restaurant in the United States, "El Torito" offered up an Aug. 24, 1999 press release touting "The warm display of Mexican hospitality" in its restaurants.

This hospitality is in keeping, the release says, with the fact "El Torito features the most enticing south-of-the-border traditions."

There is some possibility that this would not be the case, that people would not know they are enjoying the "authentic" food and spirit of Mexico and its people unless they are told. They might think they were simply in a Mexican restaurant in the United States having something to eat.

But such isolated acts—free from a broader "salsafication" of one's non-Hispanic spirit and the resonating harmonies of a spicy, Hispanic world—are not to be favored.

The restaurant is, after all, competing with other chain Mexican restaurants claiming to be offering genuine Hispanic food and spirit— and with anyone in the business of "salsafying" non-Hispanics from other kinds of "salsafied" products, a concern since spicy Hispanic spirit has become so homogenized and available in a host of products and entertainments.

And, at this point, consumers seem to have "gotten the message," and to want not only the meal—from, in this instance, the chain Mexican restaurant but also the metaphorical meatiness that goes along with it.

The promotion by "El Torito" is of a complete "world" of meaning, an encounter with a richly resonant region of fiesta spirit, fiesta elements, and fiesta place (namely, Mexico, for the restaurant).

The restaurant is not just "in lieu of the place," it is *like the place*, or so it presents itself.

Everything about the visit to "El Torito"—as the press releases proudly trumpet over time—is intended to deepen and harmonize the evocations of the "salsafied" Hispanic world.

The "fiesta furnishings," and "contemporary Mexican décor," for example—touted in an October 18, 1999 press release entitled "El Torito Spices Up Northern California With a New Restaurant"—are only part of the "El Torito style 'Mex-perience'" helping to make the imaginative journey to the Hispanic world possible, a world in which a fiesta is always going on and the happy Hispanic Fiesta People are perennially partying with hedonistic abandon.

For one's convenience, most of the chain's restaurants are located in the United States, and for practical reasons, the restaurants' personnel might not all come from Mexico, or might not—at every restaurant, again reflecting the personalities of the people at each restaurant—uniformly offer the same vibrancy and authenticity of Hispanic spirit.

But this is not what "El Torito" says. Hispanic spirit—the high-level hospitality of the Mexican variety—has been, in effect, "captured" by "El Torito" from the physical place of Mexico and "brought to" the chain's restaurants, which apparently function as little oases of the "salsafied" Hispanic world from which one can leave refreshed and ready to face the real world again. For one will be armed with Hispanic fiesta spirit, temporarily transported into the Hispanic world and, if all goes as "El Torito" hopes, temporarily transformed into a "surrogate" Hispanic able to commune on some metaphorical level with real Hispanics *somewhere* who are having the same kinds of sensory and emotional sensations. There may be Hispanics, as diners themselves, in the restaurant, but they are not vital to one's imaginative projection into the Hispanic world and the shared sensory sensations one is having (as a non-Hispanic) with those unseen Hispanics. They might help, but are unlikely to be able to compete with the Hispanics of the "mind's eye," created, in large part, by pop culture's portrayals of Hispanics-As-The-Fiesta-People.

Helping more might be the waiters and waitresses (including any Hispanic ones) whose own self-interest (in terms of the "tip" to be gained) is at stake as they try to help people's "salsafication" experience to be a successful one.

It may not be talked about—may not merit a mention in "El Torito" pronouncements to the world—but there is here a meeting, a convergence, of two great stereotypes in America.

One, of course, is Hispanics-As-The-Fiesta-People, eager to share their enlivening spirit with people who have not been blessed by birthright as a Hispanic to have such hedonistic spirit.

The other is that white people are fundamentally lacking such spirit, and the terms applied to many white Americans (often by other white people) are explicative of this viewpoint—"workaholics," "anal-retentive," "cold," among others.

Pop culture is simply bringing the two spirits together for some spiritual communing and transformation.

"El Torito" adds some Mexican food to the "transfer," food that is, of course, symbolic of, and substantially "containing" the Hispanic spirit of value to white and other non-Hispanic Americans.

Carping about things like discrimination, or lack of federal funding for Hispanic programs, *does* seem small indeed when larger issues like the morale and spirit of the entire country are at stake. Especially when everyone else is celebrating Hispanic culture and even offering, in this way, a kind of political support for Hispanic people and Hispanic *countries*.

"Every scent and every spice in an 'El Torito' kitchen shouts 'Viva Mexico,'" says a Sept. 29, 1999 press release from the chain.

No wonder another Mexican restaurant chain, Taco Bell, adopts a "Revolution" campaign—the one featuring the Mexican Chihuahua, begun several years ago. The next wave of people supporting Hispanic culture, fighting for their place in American society (and for *their* place inside the Mexican restaurants or in the drive-thru lines) will be the new generations of non-Hispanic Americans.

They will be the strongest "Hispanic culturalists"—and as the "Fiesta Culture" becomes an even more indelible part of mainstream American culture, their fervor for Hispanic food and other cultural elements ("channeled" and "encouraged" by popular culture's "salsafied" Hispanic model) comes to seem an expression of American patriotism itself.

A spirit infinitely exportable, it appears, and perhaps some of the future, fevered boosters will be non-American, non-Hispanics.

A May 28, 1998 press release from "El Torito" Restaurants announced that the chain would "develop" 21 restaurants in the Middle East, joining an international complement (at the time) of seven "El Torito" restaurants in Japan and one in Turkey.

This, of course, is in addition to the Taco Bell chain's fast-food restaurants located in some 20 foreign countries.

And the enthusiasm for Mexican food, the near obsessive desire for it (as well as other Hispanic 'salsafied" products)? Well, if it hasn't yet reached the level of obsession, pop culture is doing its level best to enlist its adherents in such fanatical, "revolutionary," devotion approaching (and maybe even arriving at) addiction.

"El Torito fans soon will be able to get their Mexican food *fix* (italics added) at the local supermarket," according to a Jan. 10, 1998, release from the company. "The 69-unit restaurant chain will sell salsa, salad dressing, taco kits and other products through a licensing pact with Hormel Foods Corp. of Austin, Minn."

(It is unclear whether this arrangement has borne out, but—as with birthday presents—it's the thought that counts when it comes to Hispanic Resonance.)

For the "Sensory Search" only works as well as it does when non-Hispanic Americans *believe* in it as a means to their imaginative projection into underlying Hispanic harmonies.

"Taco Bell" and "Dinky, The Talking Chihuahua"

No consideration of the "Sensory Search," of America's "salsafication" more broadly, is complete without a somewhat more detailed examination of "Taco Bell" than our brief mentions to this point.

To begin with, there are just so many of them—nearly 6,700 in 2002 of this chain's fast food Mexican restaurants across America, serving (according to the company) more than 35 million consumers each week. The Feb. 10, 2002 edition of "60 Minutes" on CBS—in a

69

segment on fast food—noted how "Taco Bell Express" outlets were now located *inside* some schools' cafeteria operations.

Its role in non-Hispanic Americans' "salsafication" from tangible Hispanic fiesta elements is undeniable.

And Taco Bell's share of the Hispanic Resonance used by popular culture is also considerable.

Taco Bell folds Hispanic Resonance—the perennial part of it represented by the "Escape to Mexico" or other parts of the Hispanic "world"—into its appeal.

The chain's "Make A Run For The Border" ad campaign of recent years effectively made use of this "Escape to Mexico" evocation.

The ads played off the idea in Hispanic Resonance of Mexico as *Sanctuary*, as a "shelter" for one's sensory awakening and exploration.

All those times in a movie when (usually) white Americans are yearning to be in Mexico, they're really (apparently) hungering to be enjoying the sensory sensations of the fiesta elements available there.

And, depending on when the movie was made, the characters in question are poignantly anticipating the onset of an America dotted with Taco Bells and other chain Mexican restaurants or filled with supermarkets selling frozen Mexican food.

This "escape" can also include "time-travel."

With its architectural mission motif—and the distinctive "Mission Bell" atop the entrance to each of its chain restaurants—Taco Bell has sagely put the resonance of the Hispanic past into play.

Taco Bells remind us of the connection between landscape and "memory," between the built environment and our sense of heritage and legacy.

And what "Taco Bells" suggest so powerfully is the ability (and plausibility) of America to artificially create a sense of Hispanic *place* in the built environment.

In places all around America where there is no natural Hispanic "presence" in the built environment—no Spanish missions to remind us of the legacy of Hispanic peoples who lived long ago—Taco Bells help fill the void.

In their own way—in the new "Fiesta Nation" developing in America—Taco Bells aggressively advance Hispanic Resonance in the built environment.

70

Father Junipero Serra lives again for Americans—for those Americans who fall into a happy reverie of what they learned in school about the Spanish priest who was instrumental in building the early California missions—who receive a "reminder" from Taco Bells of "history" lessons in school about the early Southwest and Spanish missions.

And maybe, sitting down with their children in a Taco Bell located hundreds or thousands of miles away from the nearest, *actual* Spanish mission (or remnants thereof), a father or mother tells them the touching story of Father Serra.

Or maybe, more likely, they talk about the Mexican Chihuahua, "Dinky," particularly in those Taco Bells and at those moments when little replicas of the Chihuahua have been available for mass distribution. "Dinky," of course, is the *Taco Bell Chihuahua*, a "spokesman" of sorts, since he "speaks" in human voice on some of the chain's commercials.

In fact, to be precise, Father Serra stories are growing less likely at Taco Bells since the chain's "mission era," so to speak, ended in 1984, when the company decided to abandon its mission-style architecture in the designs of new Taco Bells. (This leaves a lot of Taco Bells, older and unremodeled ones, with the same mission motif—and of course even the newer Taco Bells retain the distinctive mission-style "Bell" in their building designs.)

Even so, Taco Bells continue to represent Hispanic Resonance and to be an important part of America's "salsafication." And Taco Bell's success over the last few years has been especially aided by "Dinky."

We've seen how white Americans—like the "Too Hot Tamales"—can come to "personify" Hispanic spirit, helping to render Hispanic people ever more irrelevant to the process of "salsafication."

But Taco Bell shows us how animals—like a Mexican Chihuahua—can also "personify" Hispanic spirit, and can also thus speed the growing irrelevance of Hispanic people in America.

The Mexican Chihuahua in question—there is actually more than one Chihuahua used by the chain for its advertising—was originally featured on the "Revolution" campaign, with one of the first such TV "spots" showing the Chihuahua, as a kind of insurgent revolutionary figure, addressing a throng of supporters on the merits of Taco Bell offerings.

But one never knows where—or with what words—the Chihuahua will appear in the later ads to praise or pine for Taco Bell's menu items.

While the "democratizing" infrastructure of "salsafication"—with the development and spread of chain Mexican restaurants, among other things—reaches across America, this should not (as we have said) imply a corresponding increase in the "need" for Hispanic-Americans to help non-Hispanic Americans achieve "surrogate" Hispanichood.

Except for the fact that "Dinky," the Taco Bell Chihuahua, *is supposed to be* a human being, according to a press release *archived* on the Taco Bell website.

In a Dec. 29, 1997 press release, the company says "Dinky" is intended to suggest a "…19-year-old guy in a dog's body…who is on an undying quest for Taco Bell."

Of course, as an actual human being, shown in the commercials instead of the Chihuahua, there would be multiple and messy complications.

The 19-year-old Hispanic man—how many non-Hispanic men would speak the heavily accented Spanish (or SalsaSpeak) "Dinky" *speaks*—would certainly be seen as a Hispanic stereotype. (Some people, including Hispanics, have no difficulty seeing "Dinky" as such a stereotype.)

And a real person would likely not be as simple to manipulate as *meaning*, as sheer piquancy amenable to reproduction in the form of, say, toys and replicas, as Taco Bell has done with "Dinky."

Besides which, a "talking" dog is lots more intriguing than a "talking" person, since people are ordinarily able to talk.

There is no doubting the sagacity of Taco Bell's choice of a Mexican Chihuahua to *represent* the character of a human 19-year-old.

"Dinky" has become a cultural icon in America, as any casual excursion into the Internet will show.

There are "fan" sites for "Dinky" and there are sites (like "E-Bay," the well-known auction website) selling "Dinky" merchandise (from t-shirts to toys).

These are "unofficial" sites not operated by Taco Bell itself. On the aforementioned official Taco Bell website, a fuller detailing, a more comprehensive iteration of the *meaning* of what Taco Bell is doing, is available.

The compelling resonance for non-Hispanic Americans of the "talking" Chihuahua appears to have even surprised Taco Bell's people, who have kept the ad campaigns featuring the Chihuahua on for longer than first planned, one learns from the Taco Bell website, for example.

And a Mexican government ad of recent vintage showed just how "influential" the Taco Bell Chihuahua has been as a Hispanic symbol.

Don't settle for fake Mexican Chihuahuas who talk, come to Mexico to see real ones, the ad said.

Whether, in fact, the best reason to go to Mexico is to see a live Mexican Chihuahua dog is debatable.

But the fact the Mexican government's tourism office believes the Taco Bell Chihuahua is so well known it makes sense to play off its resonance is noteworthy.

But be it Father Serra or "Dinky," the idea is of a Hispanic spirit every bit as savory, as inviting, as the Taco Bell food items, deepening sensory satisfactions of the food with echoes of an emotional Hispanic Resonance.

This resonance is vital in understanding the "Sensory Search," for it sharpens the direct sensation of tangible Hispanic fiesta elements like food (and drink).

It potentially makes of the simple act, say, of eating and drinking, a journey into an imagined Hispanic world.

The corporate "globalization" of the world's consumers includes Hispanic Resonance and the "Sensory Search."

As we've noted, Taco Bell has restaurants abroad in some 20 countries.

But roam as it might, Taco Bell doesn't stray very far from an essential theme of "salsafication," including offering "Fiesta Salsa" packets with its food orders.

A few extra packets and one is free to take the "Fiesta" found at Taco Bell wherever one goes.

Moreover, in one of Taco Bell's more recent ad campaigns, the Taco Bell manipulation of meaning comes under the same category of spiciness pioneered by "The Too Hot Tamales."

This effort of what *Taco Bell is trying to tell us* (regardless of what the denser among us may fail to take away from seeing those commercials) is explained in an April 24, 2001 press release. Hyping one of the latest (at the time) menu items—the "Grilled Stuft (yes, that's how they spell it) Burrito"—the release euphorically outlined how Latina model Elsa Benitez (notable for being in one of the Sports Illustrated Magazine's special swimsuit issues), appearing in a commercial to introduce the new product, exemplified the spiciness of the burrito itself.

"Elsa is the ideal spokesperson for the Grilled Stuft Burrito because she perfectly embodies the essence of the product; she's sizzling and spicy with Latin roots," the release quoted Tom O'Keefe, senior vice president and creative director of the Foote, Cone and Belding Advertising Agency.

The "progress" for Hispanics represented by the wildly successful white women known as "The Too Hot Tamales," by their *development* of the nexus between Hispanic food and Hispanic spirit, is in evidence here.

And whether the creative people at Foote, Cone and Belding who came up with this Taco Bell ad campaign featuring Benitez, the Latina model, would be willing to admit it or not, the *cultural evolution* symbolized by "The Too Hot Tamales" makes it more possible, more comprehensible, to suggest Hispanic people are exactly the same as their food.

Within limits, of course, for "The Too Hot Tamales" and the "Sensory Search" of non-Hispanic Americans for "Hispanic" sensation and spirit necessarily involve us in certain fundamental questions.

Who *are* Hispanics? How do they figure in the future of America? As a non-Hispanic, how do I come to "know" them?

As a Hispanic, what is *my place* in the nation's happy "salsafication?"

These are among the critical questions of this book, and there are certainly no more important questions for the original Fiesta People, Hispanics, and the *new, non-Hispanic Fiesta People* of America.

In this regard, "Chi Chi's" "Declaration of Salsafication" is more prescient, more reflective of pop culture's Hispanic model, than the "Chi Chi's" people may have ever intended or hoped.

Just as the "Declaration of Independence" once defined the spirit of America, and carried it forth as proudly as the "Stars-and-Stripes," this newer Declaration seems to capture the contemporary spirit of America.

Hispanic-Americans, of course, who don't celebrate this particular spirit of America, or the "salsafied" view of Hispanic culture it fosters, can be easily adjudged as unpatriotic or unfeeling. It is, after all, *their* culture that is being touted and proclaimed, triumphantly trumpeted to the nation—and the world.

The "Sensory Search" can, as we have suggested, even offer "alternative lives" to white (and other non-Hispanic) Americans.

Take Dava Sobel, for example, an award-winning (and best-selling) author of science books.

In an interview on the "Book Notes" program on the C-Span cable television channel broadcast Jan. 17, 1999, Sobel was asked by host Brian Lamb to elaborate on her mention of an interest in ballroom dance.

She explained how she had won a tango competition by giving herself the calming advice that this is "not my real life."

"...not my real life." *"Not my real life." My pretend life. My place to go when my real life doesn't give me what I need.*

Without intending to, Sobel may have spoken in this interview for millions of non-Hispanic Americans who find a "salsafying" escape from their "real lives" in Hispanic-flavored sensation and spirit, a kind of avocation of *evocation*.

The distinction to be drawn here is an important one. Sobel is obviously serious, *engaged*, in her tango endeavors and in the time she devotes to them. She likely couldn't have won a tango dance competition without being serious about the dance steps and movements involved. *It just isn't her real life.*

And not being her real life, it relieves her (and millions of other non-Hispanic Americans similarly engaged to some degree in a Hispanic "Sensory Search") of formal requirements.

Like, say, the need for actual Hispanic-Americans as a requisite part of their "self-salsafication" from tangible Hispanic elements.

SalsaSpeak, the object of our attention in the previous chapter, is critical to the "Sensory Search," to enhancing the experience of sensory sensations by adding the evocative resonance of a "salsafied" Hispanic world.

If SalsaSpeak, by itself, is a quick, "in-and-out" into Hispanic Resonance, at times—the equivalent, so to speak, of a drive-by shooting—the "Sensory Search" represents stopping at the scene of a "fiesta" to join in the enjoyment of Hispanic food, music, dance and design.

The happy pursuits of Hispanics at an imagined Ideal Fiesta—the model upon which conscientious non-Hispanics dedicated to their own "self-salsafication" depend—are considered eminently replicable.

Like the old saying about being able to "talk the talk and walk the walk," Hispanic fiesta elements—the enjoyment of which unerringly leads non-Hispanics to an experience of hedonistic Hispanic harmonies—are seen as capable of being duplicable by non-Hispanics.

If this duplicability seems (to some Hispanics, perhaps) to be duplicitous, "salsafication" in service to America, to boosting the morale and heightening the hedonistic experience of white (and other non-Hispanic) Americans, is much more important. In actual practice, anyway, although the "Private Joke"—noted in this book and earlier in this chapter as the idea of taking a deliciously ironic "salsafication" from the celebration of Hispanic spirit and elements used (in other contexts), as the basis for uncharitable stereotypes of Hispanics—appears to energize some non-Hispanics' "self-salsafications."

The particularity of the "Sensory Search" makes it seem almost superfluous to ask someone about his or her interest in actual Hispanic people. *Hey, I'm already doing everything they do* (eating Latino food, drinking Latino drinks) *and spending a lot of time and money doing it. You want me to get to know Hispanics too?* Or, *I'm already living a more authentic Hispanic life than many Hispanics* (buying Hispanic handicrafts, smoking authentic Hispanic cigars, living in a Spanish-style house) *and spending a lot of time and money doing it. You want me to spend more time just to get to know*

Hispanic people? What would I learn from them when I've already immersed myself in their culture?

The fact is, the divorce is now complete—has been for some time—and there is no particular connection (no inextricable link) between Hispanic culture and Hispanic people in American popular culture. The ability of anyone to particularize their own "Sensory Search"—from an admittedly wide range of vendors, producers, companies, and even individuals, like "The Too Hot Tamales"—makes the mediation of even a Hispanic well-versed in his rich cultural storehouse to provide any more of a greater sensory experience (and this is the level upon which Hispanic culture works its fascination for most people, anyway) a moot point. Besides, which, Hispanics who have an interest in getting to know non-Hispanics aren't like to cultivate friendships with people who only want to plumb their knowledge and experience of the Hispanic "Sensory Search."

For some white Americans, certainly, there may be some doubt as to what to talk about with Hispanics and other minorities.

That, at least, is one reason why "diversity" training is so welcome in government and non-government offices in the United States—we need to learn to "relate" to each other, to see things from the other person's point of view, even when that view may be antagonistic or, at times, antithetical to our own. That doesn't make things much easier, though. For white Americans, it is an unappetizing prospect to offer a "mea culpa"—even an internal one, to Hispanic-Americans. *For my own part, I want you to know that I'm sorry* the United States did the "Manifest Destiny" thing and took half of Mexico to create what is arguably one of the most powerful regional economic areas in the world—the American Southwest. This kind of belated "apology" seems to be the upshot of what some "multiculturalists"—the people who, at least in part, believe Americans need to come to terms with the individual components of our "melting pot"—appear to want.

Faced with a choice—one that becomes increasingly urgent in the wake of the burgeoning Hispanic population in the United States—many white Americans would prefer to opt (and have) on "The Sensory Search" as their version of exploring "diversity" and "multiculturalism."

In the next chapter, the final chapter, we will see how this personal decision by many non-Hispanic Americans is a momentous one, with serious social and political implications and *applications*.

But we have one more aspect of the "Sensory Search" to consider before moving on to the last chapter.

This part of people's pursuit of the "Sensory Search" was held in reserve while we examined the way most non-Hispanic people, probably, "discover" Hispanic sensation from the "fiesta elements."

Places Reshaped by Resonance

We are now ready to look at how the questions, the issues, posed by America's "salsafication" from the "Sensory Search" loom especially large in some places in America, cities and big portions thereof.

These are places reshaped by Hispanic Resonance, reshaped *as Hispanic Resonance*, built in the image of echoing Hispanic spirit.

It is almost a personification of Hispanic personality, what is supposed to be Hispanic personality, which is given tangible form. Becoming, in the process, a place to "hang out," to feel warmed by Hispanic spirit, replacing the need to "hang out" with actual Hispanic people for the same reason.

Places thus "morph" into evocations of Hispanic people and their essential (at their "best") fiesta spirit.

So many things become clear, the consistency of promotion and hype suddenly crystallize for one, when this is understood. The fiesta spirit is so rich, so obviously resonant in the refashioned "look" of San Antonio, Texas, for example, that just being there can allow one to experience the harmonies of the place, the things that translate into a "Fiesta Lifestyle."

Certainly, there are Hispanic people in San Antonio, but they are there (in the "Fiesta Logic" operative here) to support the overarching Hispanic Resonance.

If it was purely the people of San Antonio, the Hispanic people, who were really important, then there would be no need to so sharpen the "definition" of them, to so plainly "state" in the visual "language" of the built environment their essentiality. Said essentiality being Hispanics-As-The-Fiesta-People. And through their warming, affective spirit, Hispanics help other, non-Hispanic people—residents and (temporarily) other visitors to the city—to become surrogate Hispanics and enjoy the aesthetic harmonies of a "Fiesta Lifestyle."

And if Hispanic spirit can be found and felt by one (as a non-Hispanic) in the "fiesta architecture" of a city like San Antonio (and on a lesser scale in the efforts of other cities to "restore" Hispanic "Old Towns" into fiesta designs evoking the "salsafied" Hispanic Resonance), then it can certainly be found in non-Hispanic people. Namely, in non-Hispanic *aficionados* of Hispanic life and culture.

The power of place to be expressive of Hispanic Resonance, to memorialize its fiesta spirit in the visual landscape, and to make of it (as much as is humanly possible) a *dreamscape*, can be stunning. San Antonio's recreation of itself as a "Fiesta City" may be the pre-eminent example.

The happy daydream of the Hispanic world come to life must be a comforting reassurance that *yes, yes indeed, this is who Hispanics are.* If they built it to resemble the Resonance of Hispanics—the "best" of them—then it must all be true...the fiesta of my dreams and desires, lifting my spirit, lifting my burdens, helping me lose myself in fiesta feeling and the warming Hispanic spirit.

The way that place—rendered as Resonance—can promote a civic pride, commanding allegiance from the citizens and residents for an idea expressed in the architecture of a city, is equally expressive.

For a resident of San Antonio—a city styling itself as "The Fiesta City" (leaving one to wonder, in the wake of San Antonio's success in tourism, how many other American cities regret not having adopted the appellation first)—there must be something akin to the feeling an actor "on standby" as an "understudy" has. Or as a member of a massive community pageant (an ongoing one, every day of the week, every week of the year).

Who knows when one will be called upon to play one's part, when, say, a tourist asks for directions and one is forced to put on a "fiesta face."

And what guilt might there be if one does not, knowing how a friend or family member working in the city's considerable tourism industry depends on such allegiance to a higher community ideal by residents who are themselves "props" in a continuing "production" of the entire "Fiesta City."

At root, refusing to play one's part by putting on the "fiesta face" when the need arises, refusing to *feel* part of the ongoing fiesta of the city, is an act of civil disobedience.

For it puts in jeopardy—or would, if enough people suddenly decided not to be part of the "production"—the Hispanic Resonance that makes possible the imaginative allure of the city. And on some level of consciousness, a person living in San Antonio, a *Hispanic* person who works and pays taxes, who is concerned about the schools and the quality of life there, likely realizes the connection.

The power of place in the accelerating empowerment of Hispanic Resonance—and the attendant disenfranchisement of ordinary Hispanic human beings from the state of their own ordinariness, from the *possibility* of their own individual identity—cannot be overstated.

As confirmation of the consistency of "Fiesta Logic"—as tangible proof in the world we see (even if only on vacations or in pictures)— it puts people of common sense and of some immediate concern over the future of Hispanics in the United States on the defensive.

How can one argue persuasively against the "look" of an entire city, against the efforts of the city's officials and boosters doing their level best to so fashion the "look" of the city, without seeming unpatriotic or even dangerous?

When civic identity goes as far as it sometimes does—like in, say, the example of the El Paso Civic Center built in the shape of a giant sombrero, as it is—questioning its sanity is obviously a challenge to civil authority itself. And to the founding ideals of our nation, particularly the one about the "pursuit of happiness," this being the upshot of Hispanic Resonance to many non-Hispanic Americans in their pursuits of happiness.

Of course, even if average people are silent (or by happenstance rarely are called upon to play a supporting role in the city's constant presentation of *its* "Fiesta Face") the city's "fiesta architecture" *speaks* for them.

It represents to the world, in everything from postcards to travelogues on television, to people who actually visit and to those who only make the "virtual," vicarious visit by virtue of those postcards or travelogues, the Hispanic fiesta spirit. And it "speaks" *to* them as well. *This is what is special and distinctive about you. This is what people "like" about you.*

The "repetition," so to speak, of this message, as subtle and subliminal as it might be over time for Hispanics who live in San Antonio or the other places trying to fashion the same kind of success from putting an evocation of Hispanic Resonance in the built environment, may be significant.

To the extent that it may actually affect the way they present themselves to non-Hispanics, Hispanics can (if they consciously think about it) find an absolutely apt absurdity in the idea of "fitting in" in a community being physically reshaped to evoke Hispanic Resonance.

CHAPTER 4

THE "FIESTA" AS PUBLIC POLICY RESPONSE

"Since our Nation's founding, Hispanic Americans
have played an integral role in our country's
exceptional story of success…Today Hispanic culture
continues to shape the American experience…All
Americans, regardless of national origin, celebrate the
vibrant Hispanic American spirit that influences our
Nation's art, music, food, and faiths…"
—From the official Proclamation of National
Hispanic Heritage Month by President George W.
Bush, Sept. 2001

The social and political "applications" of "salsafication"—its
amazing adaptability to meet changing national needs and
challenges—elevate the "fiesta" to a new place of prominence in
American life.

This is the "Fiesta As Public Policy Response," the "fiesta" as
answer to any problems posed by a more Hispanic America. A
country becoming more heavily populated by Hispanics, that is, as the
2000 Census showed.

And talking about the 2000 Census' Hispanic findings—as the
Cable News Network (CNN) did in March 2001 in a report by
Correspondent Susan Candiotti—they could be seen as a measure of
the nation's deepening "salsafication."

The CNN report gushed over the increase in the Hispanic
population.

Americans love Hispanic culture, the report enthusiastically
advised.

For these more recent Hispanic arrivals to America, the CNN
report had a clear message…

Welcome to the "Fiesta" *already in progress* in America.

The suggestion of a generally smooth transition into the new land
of America for the newer Hispanic immigrants was, however, folded

into a more profound idea at work here in terms of the Hispanic presence in America more generally.

This presence includes, of course, Hispanics whose forebears have been here for *generations* or even *centuries*.

And this more profound idea?

Namely, the greater American reckoning with Hispanics has taken place. And "salsafication" has successfully emerged from the encounter between the Hispanic and non-Hispanic peoples of the country.

The import of this CNN report, of the major "Storyline" involved, is thus to update us on the evolution of American history to this point, to the status Hispanics have achieved in America.

It is, apparently, as *enablers* of the freedom Americans have to choose from an ever-greater variety of sensory sensations from "salsafying" Hispanic elements.

More Hispanics will thus mean a further enriching, a greater *enabling*, of non-Hispanic Americans' opportunities to tailor their "self-salsafications" from Hispanic elements like food and music.

And it becomes further "evidence" of the legitimacy—*as logic*—of "salsafication" as a *social movement* in support of Hispanic-Americans.

As the popularity of "salsafied" Hispanic products and entertainments grows, so too does this "proof" of success of millions of ordinary Hispanic-Americans as measured by America's spreading "salsafication."

Thus, the series of replies able to be given to Hispanics who question America's (and non-Hispanic Americans') commitment to its Hispanic people are growing apace with the nation's "salsafication."

What do you mean, Hispanics aren't succeeding? Do you know how many music albums Ricky Martin has sold in his career?

What do you mean, the government isn't doing anything for Hispanics? We have an official Hispanic Heritage Month celebration every year!

We have now entered into the realm of an absurdity—a series of absurdities, actually—applied to America's future, to the kind of people and country we are becoming.

America's Story is being rewritten, revised in the wake of our national "celebration" of Hispanics-As-The-Fiesta-People, and in the malleable *meaning* it has for those eagerly exploiting, *expropriating* it for their own mercenary aims.

We will look at how this *Story* of America's "salsafication" is reshaping journalism and commerce, politics and language. And even our very thought and perception about things having nothing directly to do with Hispanics.

Our examination will, of necessity, show how the distinctions between, say, journalism and politics, are blurring.

For the kind of journalism which covers Hispanics-As-The-Fiesta-People, a "Fiesta Journalism," fits comfortably with a politics and politicians who court Hispanic voters by holding little *fiestas* of their own, or who happily show up at Hispanic Heritage events to laud Hispanics for their great spirit and culture.

We will, in this chapter, offer a "case study" of "Cinco de Mayo" and its relevance to the accelerating development and visibility of "Fiesta Journalism" and its political corollary, the "Fiesta As Public Policy Response."

We will also explore how the "public policy debate" on serious national issues having no direct connection to Hispanics—like the transition of presidential power—is being trivialized and distorted by *Hispanic Resonance* and *SalsaSpeak*.

This last phenomenon holds great danger for non-Hispanics and for our country, for it strikes at the very idea of democracy as defined (in part) by an informed citizenry.

But this appears to be no deterrence to politicians or journalists who see an immediate—even inspiring—benefit to the fiesta as *meaning*, to "salsafication" as the latest unfolding and flowering of *America's Story*.

"Salsafication" as Story

"Salsafication's" qualities as Story, as narrative, are compelling.

It takes the unwieldy facts of all these individual Hispanics coming to the United States and gives this story shape, structure. Even if one—as a non-Hispanic American—is not seeking after a "self-salsafication," one can still certainly understand this "Storyline."

And for those white (and other non-Hispanic) Americans who are so engaged (at times, anyway), this "Storyline" is a comforting, reassuring one.

For the idea of the *meaning* of all these Hispanic immigrants is completely absorbed by these non-Hispanics long before the immigrants themselves will ever be fully integrated into American life.

This *Story* of Hispanics as a greater, more colorful backdrop for non-Hispanics' "self-salsafications" from Hispanic spirit and sensation (or more precisely, what is perceived to be Hispanic spirit and sensation) is an eloquently evocative one.

And it is a kind of "organizing principle," of *control*, of course, over these bare facts, imbuing them with meaning for reporters and commentators alike—the *Storytellers* in the popular media.

This "organizing principle" is not completely successful, not completely encompassing, as the continued currency of blatantly "negative" Hispanic "Storylines" on television and movies shows.

But it is still an important one, and growing more important all the time as Hispanic numbers increase and the incentive to see Hispanics as non-threatening (and to convince Hispanics of their happy *role* in America) also increases.

This control over mental "materials" does have a corollary in "real-world" applications.

The expectation of newer Hispanic arrivals to America acquiescing to this idea of their "place" in America carries within it a ready rejection (figuratively speaking) of those Hispanics who see themselves differently.

These Hispanics are, to put it plainly, "party poopers."

And in this popular "Storyline," there is no "place" for "party poopers."

For, the *reasoning* goes, this is a "salsafication" so substantive, so *spectacular*, it can effectively deal with Hispanic people's problems and aspirations.

If Hispanics suffer from the effects of prejudice and discrimination, "salsafication" offers the solution.

When non-Hispanics get to "know" Hispanic life and culture—as they can from the fiesta elements of food (and drink), music, dance and design—they will begin to "understand" and accept them.

"Salsafication" is easily employed, as the need arises, as a politics that works—which makes a difference in people's lives—for Hispanics in America.

And the need is arising now.

It is, in fact, insurgently *emergent*.

The 2000 Census—with its release in 2001 of the Hispanic population numbers, as we have mentioned—has only spurred this newer use of the *meaning* of "salsafication."

The political applications of this *story* involving Hispanics play off one pre-eminent premise—Hispanic-Americans will be so caught up in the happy "celebration" of their culture and spirit by non-Hispanics they will fail to see the obvious. They will decide *not* to be "party poopers."

Unfortunately, their powers of perception and reason will be weakened to the degree they "buy into" the logical underpinnings of the national "salsafication." To wit...

Their enjoyment of the fiesta elements of food (and drink), dance, music and design will take on profounder overtones *for them*.

As the *first* "constituency"—in an almost literal political sense—of the most visible "salsafied" products and entertainers, Hispanic-Americans can even be deceived into believing "salsafication" *is* a *social movement* empowering them.

And that their "support" of these products and entertainers will spur this *movement* and speed the better day it heralds for all Hispanic-Americans.

This "Storyline"—adopted for calculated political purposes by ever more people—seems inordinately capable of lulling Hispanics into a willing suspension of reality to believe in its "happy ending."

When the vast majority of non-Hispanic Americans have been "salsafied" from Hispanic sensation and spirit, their natural sympathies and support for Hispanics will practically end discrimination and guarantee Hispanics' participation in every part of American life, this happy ending "goes."

The novelty of "belonging" may be the final nudge for at least some Hispanic-Americans.

It could not be a more powerful narrative, whose poignant re-telling may vary from politician to politician—depending on their eloquence and apparent sincerity—but which nonetheless "speaks" to

Hispanic yearnings every bit as compelling as those of non-Hispanics for their "self-salsafications."

Hispanics who finally feel like they *belong* in America, like they are being accorded a respect and affection from white (and other non-Hispanic) Americans they *don't even know* (from the media reports reaching them of non-Hispanics' immersion in Hispanic culture) may desperately want to believe in this "happy ending."

They "know" they have to be patient for "salsafication's" final fruition—to perhaps only help their children and future Hispanic generations—but it may effectively substitute (in *some* of their minds) for individual social action and political activism on their part.

Of course, there is no "happy ending" here for Hispanics in this *Story*.

America's big "Bienvenido" to new Hispanic residents of the United States is a happy absurdity.

Hispanics are to be welcomed—as made clear in the CNN report—because of their culture, which non-Hispanics love and are enjoying, principally through the "fiesta elements" of food, music, dance and design.

But if non-Hispanics already are enjoying readily available Hispanic fiesta elements, then more (or any, actually) Hispanics aren't needed.

Their role as bearers of the necessary Hispanic Resonance—vital to non-Hispanics' "self-salsafications"—can be played (at this point in the evolution of Hispanic Resonance, anyway) just as well outside the United States.

In fact, better, because actual Hispanic human beings in the United States are always capable of being, at any moment, complicated or contrary human beings (okay, "party poopers") unbefitting their "fiesta mold" in the "salsafied" version of Hispanic life and culture.

Any requirement for the direct presence or proximity of Hispanic human beings to non-Hispanics' "self-salsafications" has been plausibly overcome by the actual practice of American pop culture.

The Hispanic spirit—the ultimate source of "salsafication" for non-Hispanics—inhering in concentrated form (*Hispanic Extract*, like vanilla extract) in pop culture's "salsafied" Hispanic-style products, like Mexican food items commercially sold *everywhere* in the United States, ably replaces actual Hispanic people.

And there are all the other elements of the "fiesta infrastructure," which can be given a political application to foster Hispanics' belief in the "happy ending."

Welcome to the "Fiesta Country"

New Hispanic immigrants to the United States will find a *Fiesta Country* awaiting them, *surrounding* them, if they so choose. They can drive a *Ford Fiesta* car, paint their house with *Fiesta Orange House Paint*, and shower with *Fiesta Splash Body Wash* from *Zest*.

They can watch the *Fiesta Bowl*, reveling in the great Hispanic spirit being transferred to the non-Hispanic members (most, if not actually all) of the "Fiesta Dancers" troupe in the *Fiesta Bowl Parade*.

They can patronize "Taco Bell" and get extra packets of the chain's *Fiesta Salsa*, to use at home at times when they can't conveniently visit this fast food restaurant.

They can participate in their local *fiestas*, held during Hispanic Heritage Month or at other times of the year.

The clear evidence of this blossoming (supposedly) respect and affection for Hispanics, of course, includes the way Hispanic entertainers are treated.

Some of these entertainers, certainly, are seen as cultural icons, revitalizing America's very spirit, spearheading the budding acceptance of diversity by non-Hispanic Americans. Sadly, this "happy ending" is a shameless effort (for broader commercial and political purposes) to involve Hispanics in the absurdity of "celebrating" the stereotype of Hispanics-As-The-Fiesta-People.

It may have been polished up a bit, it may have been given an evocative entry into the social and political future of the country, but it is still a stereotype, a generalization, a trivial and trivializing distortion.

Of course, this *social movement* for Hispanics is not what "salsafication" means, at least initially, on the "front lines" all over America as white and other non-Hispanic Americans become more aware of Hispanics and their culture.

However, the political *meaning* of "salsafication" as broader *American Story* is clearly built, in large part, on the "knowledge" gleaned by non-Hispanic Americans from their sensory sensations of Hispanic elements like food.

Take, for example, the sincerity of an elderly white woman—who so identified herself—calling the C-Span cable channel's "Washington Journal" program on the morning of Mar. 19, 2001 during a "Hispanic Issues" segment. On this day, C-Span had posed a question to its viewers on the meaning for America of the rapid growth of the Hispanic population, revealed by the then just-released figures from the 2000 national U.S. Census.

The female caller couldn't be more pleased.

It would be very beneficial to non-Hispanic Americans, she said.

Already, she noted, the increase in Hispanics among the residents of her area had resulted in the local supermarket stocking more Hispanic food items, a boon to her and her non-Hispanic family members who so enjoy Hispanic food.

If this is what the growth of the Hispanic population means to non-Hispanic Americans—a greater choice of sensory stimulations and satisfactions—they are all for it.

The clear earnestness of the woman could not be mistaken.

In her mind, she was voicing support for a changing America, for a more Hispanic America.

This she did willingly, happily, to the extent of calling (for her) one of the long-distance, *non-toll-free*, telephone numbers of C-Span set up to receive callers' comments as part of the program's format.

The political *message* of "salsafication" thus does appear to be getting through to average non-Hispanic Americans.

The particular permutation here was the *immigration* of Hispanics to America, and the *spread* of the Hispanic population to more areas within the country (ergo, the white woman's joy Hispanics had finally arrived in her little part of America to prompt an addition to the local supermarket's inventory).

This is a great example, from a "Hispanic Issues" segment—as superimposed on the screen—on the C-Span "Washington Journal" program, of the disembodied Hispanic spirit, *Hispanic Resonance*, replacing Hispanic people.

Another C-Span caller—during a "Diversity" segment on the "Washington Journal" a few days after the Journal's "Hispanic" segment—took an even more practical stand on the meaning of more Hispanics in America.

Hispanic farm workers made possible the wide availability of vegetables for Americans to eat, and she was grateful. One can easily imagine a subdividing of the saying of "Grace"…"Thank You God for giving us Hispanics to pick the vegetables we enjoy today…"

Or equally poignant scenes in which white (and other non-Hispanic) people at community meetings called to defuse racial and ethnic tensions defend their sensitivity toward Hispanics by citing how some of their most familiar and comforting sensory sensations and experiences are Hispanic ones…

"We had a piñata for my grandchild's birthday party," an older white man says, looking around at the unfamiliar faces of some of the many Hispanics who are his new neighbors, among the people at this community forum. *"Would I have done that if I didn't like Hispanics?"*

The fact is—as "salsafication" has so supremely shown us in actual practice—the greater enjoyment of Hispanic "culture" with larger numbers of Hispanics in the United States has no requisite need for any actual contact with Hispanic people.

For the C-Span caller we have cited first, the Hispanic products in the supermarket do quite nicely in terms of satisfying an interest in what Hispanic culture has to offer.

For the Hispanic people *are there*, in the products, metaphorically speaking.

Their sauciness and piquancy—all the things they would offer in person to non-Hispanics—have been *concentrated into* the "salsafied" products so widely available.

The complications of Hispanic people coming from so many different countries with their separate histories and cultures and flags and national anthems may make it seem easier to mediate one's "knowledge" of Hispanics through one's sensory sensations.

U.S. News and World Report magazine offered, in its May 11, 1998 issue, an article headlined "'Hispanics' Don't Exist," summarized (in part) on the table of contents page with the line "America's fastest-growing ethnic group isn't an ethnic group at all."

90

Of course, it's not the idea they don't exist. It's the idea—as the *U.S. News and World Report* article went on to detail—that so many of them exist from differing national societies (and the subgroups within even individual nations).

This is such a withering assault on the idea of Hispanics as a single social and political force, it can serve a political purpose for some as the Hispanic population increases.

But the *momentum* of this time in America—and "salsafication" is certainly a *defining momentum* in our country—is not with the idea of differentiating Hispanics.

This idea of exploring the differences within and between Hispanic subgroups would not fit the happy *daydream* of "salsafication," would not fit naturally into the simple confines of this newer *Story of America*.

We will now look at specific sectors, like the media, and how they are using America's "salsafication" from Hispanic sensation and spirit for their own purposes.

There is, of course, no more important group in this regard than business people.

In the previous chapter on non-Hispanics' *Sensory Search* in the Hispanic "world," we saw how marketers of *fiesta elements* like food are absolutely frenzied in their promotion of "salsafying" Americans' tastes and spirits.

But we are here concerned with social and political issues, and it is in this context we look to the companies targeting *Hispanic* consumers, and their "contributions" to co-opting Hispanics.

In a consumer culture, large numbers of Hispanics are also seen as powerful, able to wield their group "purchasing power." Marketers are using an aggressively applied "salsafication" as *meaning* to win Hispanic-Americans to their particular products and brands.

As with politicians who market themselves to Latinos, companies deliberately appealing to Hispanics are *responding* to Hispanics as "voters" in the marketplace who have the "choice" of where to spend their money.

By showing they are "supporting" the *institutions* of Hispanic-American life—advertising on Spanish-language television in the United States with "culturally-sensitive" commercials, for example—the companies make the pitch they are *for* Hispanics. And—as it neatly folds Hispanics into an *American Dream* of happy consumers—this fact is also given a political cast.

You're powerful. Taken together, you represent hundreds of billions of dollars of purchasing power. This means America has to "listen" to you, to take you seriously.

Much of the theoretical work here has been done by advertising agencies, by people eager to sell Hispanics the things they need to fully realize their potential as participants in a material American culture, a consumer culture.

And what these marketers are "hearing," what they're telling corporations who would do business with Hispanic consumers, goes something like this...

"Hispanics want to see their lives portrayed in a sympathetic way, to feel like the things they're buying are part of their 'assimilation' in America."

Thus, corporations too can become part of the *social movement* of "salsafication," and anyone who pays some attention to Hispanic-directed advertising (like that on U.S. Spanish-language television) quickly sees how this message of enjoying a festive Hispanic life is intimately tied to becoming a good American consumer. A beer commercial on Spanish-language television here in America is as likely as not to be a *fiesta* with friends and family, a welcome reward for the hard work of building a life in America.

This sort of advertising is in line with the traditional idea of changing the Hispanic "image" presented by movies, television and other media.

Enlisting Hispanics In Their Own Trivialization

But as we've noted, this effort is simply one of enlisting Hispanics in their own trivialization.

Even when, as in one Miller Beer commercial in 2001, Hispanics are portrayed as in ascendancy in America.

The setting for this TV spot is a baseball stadium where a small Latino man is standing next to a tall, heavyset white man in the bleachers as the National Anthem is being played.

The Latino remarks to the other man about how baseball is the great American pastime, as the camera pans over the players standing on the field for the National Anthem as well, the back of their jerseys showing their distinctly Hispanic surnames.

Superimposed on the television screen at the close of the commercial: *Es Su Tiempo, Es Tiempo Miller*.

Translated literally—"It's Your Time, It's Miller Time."

Obviously, the literal words are the lead-in here to what the commercial (and the beer company sponsoring it) *can't say*.

What exactly is it about this time that makes it Hispanics' time? The fact they are the largest minority? Black Americans will tell you this fact alone doesn't automatically make it a group's "time."

A few Latino baseball players? The hype about Hispanics? Hispanics' purchasing power in general, or ability to buy beer in particular?

And if it is truly Hispanics' "time," does the beer company have the *blueprint*, the *plan,* available to any Latino who buys, say, a case of Miller Beer, on how to make the most of *this time in America favoring Hispanics* before it's over?

Probably not.

Almost certainly not. Miller Beer is in the beer business, not the Hispanic empowerment business.

But this is a strange moment in America and everyone, from elderly, white ladies happy Hispanics are prompting changes at the local food store to beer companies hailing the *Hispanic Time* in America, is welcome at the ongoing *National Fiesta*. Hispanic entertainers also manage quite nicely to meld their self-interest in America's "salsafication" to the larger theme of it as *social movement* for Hispanics.

Taking pride—as a Hispanic-American—in the energizing of the country, of very many individual non-Hispanic Americans, from Hispanic sensation and spirit becomes a patriotic act in the *logic* in play here.

This is why the support by Hispanic entertainers especially for "salsafication" as model and measure of Hispanic "progress" in America is so alarming.

These entertainers offer a *validation* of the ideas informing "salsafication," of its values and benefits for ordinary Hispanic-Americans.

93

This becomes particularly significant in *Fiesta Journalism* and for politicians' use of the "Fiesta As Public Policy Response." And in this regard there may be no better example than Gloria and Emilio Estefan, tour de force entrepreneurs and "salsafication *theorists*" as much as entertainers.

The enlivening spirit of the Estefans' music (Gloria as singer, Emilio as producer in recent years, since his "retirement" from performing in public with Gloria) with the "message" in some of the song lyrics about spicy Latin culture and its *transferability* to everyone (including, obviously, non-Hispanics), is one of their hallmarks.

Their vision of Hispanic success in the future is of the greater participation of Hispanics in the *presented story* of America and Americans in movies, television, music and other entertainment venues, as Emilio Estefan has detailed in interviews with, among others, the CNN cable channel.

But the Estefans take their "act," so to speak, into the "public arena," exploiting the idea of Hispanic entertainers as personifications of the idealized, "salsafied" Hispanic spirit, as "representatives" of the Hispanic community. The Estefans take this idea of the order of things very seriously. And their direct application of it to their own lives and interests is a highly instructive "lesson" in the broader story of America's "salsafication" we are examining here. And of the fact it ultimately has nothing to do with Hispanic progress and empowerment (outside of, say, a few Hispanics like the Estefans who help in non-Hispanic Americans' "self-salsafications").

For the Estefans, the crafting of "image" and the promotion of America's "salsafication" have been part of a conscientious, and at times strikingly skilled, effort over time.

When the Florida Mariners baseball team—in the World Series for the first time a few years ago—were battling not only the Cleveland Indians baseball team but also the cold weather of Cleveland, Ohio, Gloria Estefan sent "help."

Help in the form of authentic Hispanic food dispatched by air courier service from Miami to the members of her hometown Mariners, a move that received wide "play" in the news.

The stress on the idea of *authentic* Hispanic food being sent to the Mariners' *beisboleros* (some of whom were, in fact, Hispanic) didn't seem accidental, as different news organizations played up this part of the story.

But this was—and is—only a modest tribute to authenticity by the Estefans when compared to their *developmental* work on the "Bongo's" nightclub, situated inside "Disney World," in Orlando, Florida.

This 500-seat nightclub is nothing so much as homage to the resonance of Hispanic authenticity, specifically to the era—now decades past—when the Cuban big-band "sound" became a featured part of some of America's most sophisticated nightspots. Cuban bandleaders like Xavier Cugat and Desi Arnaz—yes, the "Ricky Ricardo" of the "I Love Lucy" show—were among the well-known leaders of this cultural renaissance of Latin music, and it is their spirit which is mined to help create the *atmosphere* and milieu of "Bongo's."

This is what the Estefans and their people have said about why they brought "Bongo's" forth. And Disney's executives have been happy to sign on to supporting the re-creation of the intimacy of 1940's-era nightclubs with a 500-seat club within the Disney World complex.

In their vision of how the world should be organized, the Estefans help to "represent" the great Hispanic spirit and culture to non-Hispanics on behalf of millions of ordinary Hispanic-Americans.

But Gloria Estefan, who decided to "speak out" on the *issue* of Elian Gonzalez, finally found herself speaking out on the *issue* of Hispanic spirit. Elian, you'll recall, was the little Cuban boy rescued in November 1999 off the shores of Florida after escaping from Cuba with his mother (who had died in the attempt) and others in a leaky boat.

When public opinion turned markedly against Cuban-Americans vociferously supporting the effort to allow Elian Gonzalez to stay in the United States, Estefan felt forced to make a public statement about how Americans needed to make a distinction about Cuban-Americans' emotion and any propensity for violence (which Estefan said was not something Americans should fear from Cuban-Americans).

The self-same Hispanic spirit helping to power America's "salsafication," catapulting the Estefans to the summits of the entertainment industry and success, could just as seamlessly boomerang back on the Estefans (or any Latino who takes the idea of "salsafication" as *social movement* for Hispanics seriously).

Gloria Estefan, taking advantage of a "Fiesta Journalism" that thrives on the use of Hispanic entertainers as "leaders" of the Hispanic community, found herself a victim of it.

For "Fiesta Journalism" is no happy helper of Hispanics in America.

It is, rather, a fan of the simplifying spirit of "salsafication," of its punchy, piquant aid in sensationalizing news coverage.

And the *Storyline* of "salsafication" as *social movement* empowering Hispanics can quickly change to accommodate the equally entertaining *Storyline* of Hispanics themselves as "too salsafied," threatening the order of society.

The fact is, *this* "Storyline" is *always* available, for it is the *Hispanic Resonance* that makes possible "salsafication" itself.

The strong echoes of this trivializing generalization also figure prominently in politicians' use of "salsafication" as *social movement* for Hispanics.

The national political agenda can comfortably handle only a certain number of issues commanding politicians and people's attention. And there is little apparent desire to undertake the kind of soul-searching examination America has undergone (and still undergoes) with the last largest minority—black Americans. Instead, we have the "Fiesta-As-Public-Policy-Response" for Hispanics-The-Fiesta-People.

The more sinister reading of politicians' deliberate effort to appeal to Hispanic voters on the basis of an affection for Hispanic culture is of Hispanics as a *unique* voting bloc. This is a view of Hispanics as distrustful of the candidate armed with all the facts and figures but lacking "corazon" (heart).

If Hispanics can't make an emotional connection with the candidate, this theory goes, then they will be less likely to vote for him (or her) than the more pragmatic, non-Hispanic voters of the country.

The candidacy, at the time, of the current President of the United States, George W. Bush, is a direct example.

In the 2000 campaign, Bush made great pains to make the *emotional* connection with Hispanic voters, speaking Spanish to Hispanic audiences, for example.

Bush "speaking your language" became, for reporters and pundits, Bush "speaking" to the *issue* of Hispanics' concerns for the preservation of their culture and language.

Developed out for more detailed consideration, however, this was simply a way to "invest" a superficial issue with an evocative resonance.

Millions of Hispanics living in the United States, many of them speaking Spanish as their first language, could be poignantly assured Bush "understood" them, literally and figuratively. When Bush spoke Spanish on the campaign trail, reporters were more impressed with this fact (for the reasons just mentioned) than they were with *what* he said.

Of course, Bush wasn't generally saying anything particularly significant—or specific—in his Spanish-language remarks.

He wasn't saying things like "We will combat the terrible dropout rates from high school among Hispanic students, even if we have to spend *billions of dollars* to do it."

Instead, he would typically speak of his affection for Hispanics and their culture, of the fact he had Hispanic relatives (by virtue of his brother Jeb Bush's marriage—with children—to a Mexican woman), and his *policy* of inclusiveness.

Bush also proved, during the 2000 presidential campaign, he would be (if elected) a president eminently able to preside over a country, a *people*, eagerly engaged in a "salsafication" from Hispanic spirit and culture.

Appearing on the "Oprah Winfrey Show" in the closing weeks of the campaign, Bush told Oprah (in response to her question) his favorite fast food is the taco. And, he added, he was willing to make this declaration despite what anyone might think. A President willing to lead a defense of the taco, willing to proclaim his own devotion to this Mexican food item, is a president for this time in America.

But we are here concerned with Bush as someone who effectively executes a "Fiesta As Public Policy Response" approach to Hispanic voters, even when he isn't actively involved in a campaign to win Hispanic votes or when it isn't Hispanic Heritage Month (which generally goes from about the middle of September to about the middle of October).

Bush sponsored a "Cinco de Mayo" event at the White House, a little *fiesta*, in effect, featuring music and dance, on Friday, May 4, 2001. (The discrepancy of holding a celebration of May 5th on May 4th of 2001 was not due to any oversight or scheduling snafu. It was simply more convenient to the White House working with full staff on a Friday, May 4th.)

It is unclear whether the invitees were later offered culinary treats—like "nachos"—after the official program was over. In a budget-cutting move, the after-program "reception" may have been cancelled.

But it was likely more than made up for by the appearance at the event of some big-name performers (well-known to Hispanics who are interested in such things, certainly).

There was Pablo Montero, in full mariachi regalia, singing songs to the accompaniment of a live mariachi group similarly attired. (Montero was, at the time of this appearance at the White House, also appearing nightly in the taped Mexican "novella" entitled "Abrazame Muy Fuerte" (literally, "Hold Me Very Tightly")) on the U.S. Spanish-language network "Univision.")

But the most exciting part of the program, of the little "fiesta" underway on the grounds of *The White House* may have been the singing and dancing and *presence* of Thalia.

This young, pretty Mexican singer and dancer was obviously happy to be performing at the White House, excited enough herself, in fact, to depart from the mere performance to playfully pull the President's Hispanic nephew (or half-Hispanic nephew, if you want to get technical about it), George P. Bush, from the audience and dance with him.

George P. Bush, the living symbol of President Bush's vital connection to Hispanics, his extended Hispanic family.

The "Cinco de Mayo" commemoration at the White House could be considered the culmination of a political *strategy*, the successful completion of an effort to "get the message out" about Bush's *policy* toward Hispanics.

And this policy could be summed up in the way one good Hispanic, one hospitable Hispanic, would welcome another to his home. *Mi Casa, Su Casa.*

Speaking Spanish (for part of his remarks) to the assembled, invited guests seated in chairs set up on the South Lawn of the White House, Bush said the White House was the White House of all the people, including Hispanics.

It was supremely a statement of receptivity and openness to Hispanics, of *inclusion.*

Left unspoken was information on the specific policies and programs under this broader policy of *inclusion,* which would enable Hispanic-Americans to truly participate in all areas of American life.

The invited guests might have had some ideas about this, but this was not part of the program's format.

Some hint, however, of Bush's ideas about the specifics may have been offered by his choice of the people selected to stand with him in front of the audience as he delivered his brief comments.

Emilio Estefan and "Don Francisco" were the lucky ones. For "Don Francisco," the vision of America's Hispanic future is available for perusal every week in his Spanish-language "Sabado Gigante" (literally, "Giant Saturday") program broadcast to not only a U.S. audience but an international one from studios in Miami. It is a happy potpourri of music, dance, and comedy sketches interspersed with occasional travelogue snippets of "Don Francisco" hop scotching the world, and "serious" if brief examinations of topical issues.

In the United States, the program is shown on the "Univision" Network, and the "Cinco de Mayo" edition of the program helped to publicize Bush's *Hispanic policy.*

For it included not only videotaped segments from the actual White House event the day before but also an interview separately taped with President Bush inside the White House. This was "Don Francisco" as political interviewer and analyst, giving President Bush a chance to elaborate on his receptivity toward Hispanics and on the fact he has *Hispanic members of his own extended family.*

A true showman, "Don Francisco" boosted the number of attendees to an estimated 2,000 people at the South Lawn activities when he introduced the White House segment on the "Sabado Gigante" program.

This was a near ten-fold increase from the official White House announcement putting the number of invitees at little more than 200 people.

We have already alluded to Emilio Estefan's vision of America's future, in the first chapter and in this one.

But we can add here the observation it is a vision expansive enough to include even show business productions not directly developed and produced by Estefan.

Bush's *inclusion* of these two particular Hispanics at his White House fiesta to commemorate Cinco de Mayo is, of course, not to be taken as an endorsement of everything they do or believe, but it is a ringing endorsement of the idea of Hispanic entertainers and *impresarios* as "leaders" of the millions of Hispanic-Americans.

And it is certainly, on Bush's part, a ringing endorsement of the symbolism of "salsafication" and its applications to the political culture of America.

For one thing, the pop culture idea of celebrating Hispanics— Cinco de Mayo being one of the secular "high, holy days" of this celebration—is easily transferable to a political context. *By the power invested in me as President of the United States, I do solemnly affirm the "celebration" of Hispanic spirit and culture is an official one on this Cinco de Mayo*, Bush was basically saying.

And a couple of weeks later, when Bush held a White House ceremony with another set of invited guests to commemorate Cuban Independence Day, Gloria Estefan was on hand to sing the Cuban National Anthem.

Another Estefan, another Hispanic "leader" endorsing Bush by her presence and participation in the event.

(Even if Gloria Estefan's endeavor to win the hearts and minds of average, non-Hispanic Americans over to Elian's cause (and to the Cuban-Americans trying to keep him in the country) failed, it may have succeeded in further endearing the Estefans to Cuban-Americans and boosting their image as Hispanic "leaders." This certainly seems to have occurred to President Bush.)

This "evidence" of Hispanic support registers in the larger context of the nation's social and political history.

The idea of Hispanic entertainers as not only giving an "endorsement" of a political leader, but as becoming "representatives" of the Hispanic community in support of the leader in question, like, say, President Bush, is clear.

For President Bush, the impression left is an obvious one. He *must* have had some Hispanic support, future histories will likely attest.

If this seems like too speculative an interpretation of Hispanic entertainers' actions, consider the case of Ricky Martin. In the wake of his performance—his headlining, really—of a pre-inaugural party for then-President-Elect Bush, Martin suffered a rift with his personal manager.

The manager was distressed he hadn't been consulted on Martin's decision to appear, particularly since he (the manager) believed Martin's appearance would be taken as a sign of support for Bush's conservative philosophy and policies.

The benefits to politicians in our celebrity culture from such entertainers' support are hard to overstate.

George W. Bush gets to present himself as appreciating this spirit and culture, being right there with it, so to speak.

If they like me, I must be doing something right (George W. Bush thinking to himself).

Leading Latinos have given me a "stamp of approval."

And they (the Hispanic entertainers who automatically qualify as "leading Latinos") would not have achieved this station in life if they were not savvy people able to "judge" wisely of people, including political leaders.

This White House ceremony on Cinco de Mayo was not Bush's first public employment of this Mexican holiday since his heightened visibility as declared presidential candidate.

As we have said, it could be seen as the capstone of Bush's Hispanic strategy, beginning with the campaign.

The Cinco de Mayo Controversy

He had used the holiday—invoked its symbolism—to attack his Democratic opponent, then-Vice President Al Gore, for being less than caring and knowledgeable about Hispanics.

In an interview with Chris Matthews on the "Hardball" program on CNBC, on May 31, 2000, during the campaign, Bush derided Gore for (supposedly) saying "Cinco de Mayo" was Mexican Independence Day, and for telling a Hispanic audience that he, Gore, hoped his next grandchild would be born on "Cinco de Mayo."

Bush proudly told Matthews that he knew what "Cinco de Mayo" is—it commemorates a victory by Mexican soldiers and peasants over French troops in 1862 at Puebla, Mexico—and when Mexican Independence Day is.

The summary "debate" over Hispanic "issues" evinced by this "controversy" over "Cinco de Mayo" was representative of the way Hispanic Resonance and "salsafication" figured in the current President's 2000 campaign among Hispanic voters.

At the much-ballyhooed "beginning" of Bush's campaign among the nation's Hispanic voters—at an event in Michigan—Bush was flanked by little Hispanic children who were in appropriate dress for their roles at the event as Mexican folkloric dancers, giving an air of *fiesta* to the political rally.

This was followed, within a few days, by another highly publicized appearance before Hispanics in California, with what appeared to be the same little troupe of colorfully costumed Hispanic children appearing as members of a Mexican folkloric dance group at the political campaign stop.

At yet another campaign appearance with Hispanics, Bush spent much of his time happily wolfing down Mexican food with Hispanics as other Hispanics and members of the news media looked on.

The political applications at work here, the nuances of meaning that could be gleaned from these events, was certainly more than "I like a fiesta and its fiesta elements," but it included this central message as well.

Examined a little more closely, however, Bush was exercising his populism stratagem to the Hispanic electorate.

I'm one of you, I like the things you like, and I like your "culture." And even if I'm not actually Hispanic, I'm the next best thing, a man who is devoted to and knowledgeable of your culture, a "surrogate" Hispanic, in other words.

For journalists and commentators, like Chris Matthews in his "Hardball" interview with Bush (hardly a *Hardball* interview on Hispanic issues, notwithstanding), the "Cinco de Mayo" controversy was a perfect point of departure. It played off ready-made meaning, something non-Hispanics already "knew" about Cinco de Mayo. It could be concisely captured as a symbol of each candidate's Hispanic *position* and *sympathies*, without having to go into a long explanation or build a *foundation of meaning* to make this *controversy* comprehensible to non-Hispanic Americans.

And it could be used to "demonstrate" what each candidate was likely to do for Hispanics in his administration if elected. Reporters and pundits used this "Cinco de Mayo" "controversy" and similarly simplistic evidence during the 2000 campaign to *invite inferences* about the kind of job each man would do as President to help the nation's Hispanic people.

By knowing about Cinco de Mayo, Bush was showing his essential *connection* to Hispanic-Americans, was showing how he could be trusted to do right by Hispanics even if, at the moment, he was a little short on specifics about *how* he would help. Gore, on the other hand, could hardly be trusted to help Hispanics to the same degree—despite being part of an administration that had, for example, provided greatly expanded help to Hispanic education efforts—if he hadn't taken the trouble to find out what Cinco de Mayo was all about.

Gore's "surrogate" Hispanichood could be, and certainly was, questioned during the presidential campaign.

The neat substitution of an essential sympathy or "heart" for Hispanics for any specific Hispanic "agenda" on actual issues important to Hispanic-Americans was taken as substance and used as "journalism" and "commentary."

And it says a lot about how a hyped-up use of Hispanic Resonance is not only infusing the press "coverage" of Hispanics and Hispanic issues (as with the "Cinco de Mayo" controversy) but American journalism and analysis more generally.

For the ready-made *understanding* of Hispanic Resonance can also be employed to help people understand non-Hispanic people and issues, as the American media is doing its level best to demonstrate to us.

The effort to apply Hispanic Resonance to journalistic endeavors, to "salsafy" this enterprise and consider it part of the determined effort to bring people the news and make of them an informed citizenry, has far more serious implications than the heady use of SalsaSpeak by reporters and commentators.

It affects our perception and thought about "public policy" issues, about the nature of people and the world around us, about, indeed, the future of our country.

The simplification impact of "salsafication" in our popular culture, its compelling advance into political culture and American life more broadly, is a disturbing development of which Americans seem to be unaware.

A media enamored of SalsaSpeak and Hispanic Resonance is not going to regularly add "disclaimers" to its news stories and broadcasts...

Oh, by the way, we're featuring SalsaSpeak in this article (or newscast) in order to energize it, part of our broader effort to sensationalize the news coverage we provide you, and you should be aware of its mind-numbing effects...

The confluence between pop and political cultures' use of "salsafication," between the evocations of Hispanic Resonance for equally effective applications in either entertainment or serious public policy uses, appears to be accelerating.

It is, of course, a direct result of the success of "salsafication," of all the individual "self-salsafications" of white (and other non-Hispanic) Americans taking place in our country.

For these personal "encounters" with Hispanic "culture" (if not necessarily or even generally with Hispanic people as part of the process of being "salsafied") on the part of non-Hispanic Americans engaged in the exploration of Hispanic sensation and spirit build a "body of knowledge," a tangible frame of reference from which to understand Hispanic (and other) "issues."

This is the theory, at least, behind the pop/political culture nexus, the "logic" supporting the facile development of what we are here terming "Fiesta Journalism" and one of its vital parts—"Cha Cha Analysis" (such as the Chris Matthews' interview with Bush on the "Hardball" program).

The "Cinco de Mayo controversy" example we have been using has a greater meaning, has a sharper, more personal relevance, to non-Hispanic Americans because of their direct experience of the sensations of the Hispanic *fiesta elements* like Mexican food items associated with a "Cinco de Mayo" celebration.

And this kind of "knowledge" can only grow.

In contrast, in media analyses of candidates Gore and Bush at the time, the use of Hispanic issues like education for the different linguistic and cultural needs of Hispanic students might have seemed as distant for readers as, well, Hispanic people not a requisite part of their "self-salsafications."

The wholesale application of fiesta elements to considerations of our "public" life shows how America's "salsafication" goes beyond the happy Resonance of Hispanics-As-The-Fiesta-People. It can include the flip side of the *fiesta*—using, on occasion, the same fiesta elements powering the "self-salsafications" of non-Hispanic people.

Take the *pinata*.

A welcome addition to any Hispanic *fiesta* worthy of the name, the *pinata* is, of course, a brightly colored, papier-mâché construction typically made to resemble an animal (lambs are always good).

But it can also (as it so often is these days) be a symbolic stand-in for harsh criticism, particularly when leveled in the press or by political opponents against a well-known person.

On the "Rivera Live" program, on the CNBC cable channel—on Feb. 20, 2001—Paul Begala said ex-President Clinton was being treated like a *pinata* by critics upset with his pardons of certain people during the final hours of his term in office.

Eleanor Clift, a contributing editor of Newsweek magazine, used the *pinata* the very next day, Feb. 21, 2001, on "The Edge With Paula Zahn" on the Fox News Channel. She said ex-President Clinton had become everyone's "favorite *pinata*."

Clift and Begala, who assuredly know better, and more, are eloquent, erudite people who write books and are long-time savvy observers of the American political scene (and in Begala's case, a participant as well, having worked in President Clinton's White House for a time).

In order to fully appreciate the *pinata* metaphor, to take this comprehension into one's "understanding" of the issue to which the *pinata* has been linked, one needs to have seen a *pinata* in its natural habitat, a *fiesta*.

Visual SalsaSpeak can compensate for any lack of this optimal experience, optimal for the purpose of understanding the somewhat figurative use of the pinata.

In a television commercial of recent years for the American Association of Health Plans (AAHP), a *pinata* is shown being repeatedly whacked with a stick while the voice-over narration details the problem at hand.

The meaning is plain.

You don't want to be whacked around like a "pinata," do you? Well, you're going to get whacked around like a "pinata" if you don't get busy and call your Congressman.

The stripped-down symbolism—the heightening of elemental political struggle by the use of Hispanic Resonance—here brings political conflict into the realm of the comic strip (or the old "Batman" television series of the 1960's starring Adam West as the caped crusader where words like BAM!, POW! And THWACK! are actually used on the screen to denote the action) on the issue of federal legislation on health care.

This greater "salsafication" of America from a nominally fiesta element of the *pinata* is an indication of the determined (and highly-effective) appropriation of Hispanic Resonance for non-Hispanic applications beyond popular culture.

It is, in fact, an aggressively simplified approach to what are (or have traditionally been seen as) substantive issues. These are the kinds of issues that learned people at "think tanks" and universities spend their days and nights studying and analyzing to provide the information and research upon which "public policy" is typically based.

Or you can base public policy on the impact of a "pinata" commercial on voters who can create a groundswell of public opinion more influential to the federal legislators than all those highly researched, thickly bound, policy studies on the subject at hand.

This not only isn't bad—from the point of view of those who would influence elected officials of their partisan or commercial aims—it probably does make some non-Hispanics feel like celebrating Hispanics everywhere for the "contribution" of their Hispanic Resonance for such mercenary applications.

Of course—and it seems necessary to actually say it given the blurring of precision of the idea of "Hispanic *influence*" in America—the Hispanic Resonance at work today is not primarily created and maintained by Hispanics themselves.

It is happily joined in to and promoted by Hispanic entertainers, among others.

But it has been, and is now more than ever, a Resonance built up over many decades in America by stereotypes and "Storylines" about Hispanics, energizing pop culture and individual non-Hispanics' prejudices about Hispanics over the years.

The "Long Goodbye" to Hispanics becomes ever closer to completion—an ever more figurative finality—when it figures in, say, the "hand-over" of power from one non-Hispanic president of the United States to another.

In a December 2000 interview with Dan Rather on CBS as his presidency drew to a close, then-President Clinton talked about the things the incoming President, George W. Bush, should bear in mind.

In response to a question from Rather about the one movie Clinton would recommend to Bush, Clinton said he would advise Bush to watch "High Noon."

In the movie, Clinton recounted, Gary Cooper is a sheriff who must stand alone against outlaws.

And this he does, Clinton said, but not in a "macho" sort of way. Not, in other words, like the "macho" of original genesis, the "macho" of Hispanic men, although Clinton had the good grace not to so detail it in this way.

But of course he didn't have to. Hispanic Resonance has already done this for us.

This is a summing up, a "closing of the books" on the Hispanic "problem," or "question," in the United States.

Hispanics have been assimilated, in some very fundamental way, when the essence of their personality and experience, their *Resonance*, is a part of our "national dialogue" at the highest level and for the greatest of national purposes, the governing of the nation.

Our considerations are not yet complete, however, for we must still examine one more part of the "Fiesta As Public Policy Response."

"The National Fiesta"—Hispanic Heritage Month

Formalizing the *fiesta* in American life—and providing further fodder for "Fiesta Journalism"—is the officially proclaimed Hispanic Heritage Month.

As policy, it's parody, or has become so. Intended as a time when Hispanic contributions, concerns, and public policy issues could be examined and reflected upon, Hispanic Heritage Month has simply become the official "National Fiesta."

The hope of Hispanics (and their non-Hispanic allies) who pressed for a National Hispanic Heritage Week (later expanded to the current, month-long observance annually proclaimed by the President of the United States) was for a *policy focus* as a natural evolution, so to speak.

It has, instead, become an example of *arrested development*. After more than two decades of an official national Hispanic Heritage observance, the organized process implied in the word "policy"—the actual work to integrate and assimilate Hispanic Americans into American life ostensibly spurring the creation of an official observance to begin with—has not been put into place.

The broad outlines might be there in official statements, but the federal-style meaning of policy processes with built-in goals, timetables, and accountability, for empowering Hispanics and integrating them into the institutions of American life is still a fragmented and inconsistent effort.

Setting the tone for America's celebration of Hispanic Heritage Month is the statutorily mandated "Proclamation" by the President of the United States.

An annual "State of Hispanic America" report—incorporating the policy plan to bring Hispanics more fully into the life of the country—has heretofore not been an addendum to this brief Proclamation.

And there is no indication—certainly not with the "salsafication" slant of President George W. Bush—this kind of policy development will be instituted.

It is, of course, so much simpler to directly substitute the "salsafication" of America as the "assimilation" of Hispanic-Americans.

In this regard, there may be no better President for this moment in the life of the nation than George W. Bush.

Willing, as we have noted, to proclaim his favorite fast food is the taco—no matter how many people he might offend by doing so, as he said on "Oprah"—George W. Bush is a man dedicated to defending the primacy of Hispanic "culture" and elements in America.

When a presidential candidate defines, for himself, the parameters of political courage as including the defense of the taco, he is a worthy leader for the nation's Hispanic-styled "salsafication."

And the ability to transfer and adapt the meaning from one thing to another for *political* purposes will only increase in the future as Hispanics flex their political muscle.

And as (at least some) non-Hispanics seek ways to diffuse and diminish the power of Hispanic activism.

Support for live Hispanics today can, for example, be shown by "support" for long-dead ones.

At the annual *"Spanish Days"* celebration in Santa Barbara, California, the practice of dressing up like long-dead Hispanics has been part of the festive custom of the event since its inception in 1924.

For one thing, likely the main thing, it's fun.

A costume party with historical overtones in the area's past, complete with parade.

But it seems unlikely Santa Barbara—or any other place in the Southwest (or nation) with such a long-standing "tribute" to Hispanics—was an oasis of Hispanic life in the decades preceding the Hispanic civil rights struggle of more recent times.

To take a Santa Barbara *Spanish Days*—or other city's *fiesta*—out of the realm of old-fashioned fun and infuse it with a broader resonance relating to themes of Hispanic empowerment today is an outright deception.

But this is exactly what is happening.

The nation's more intense and uniform "salsafication" from Hispanic sensation and spirit seamlessly presents these events (including ones begun much more recently) as premier examples of America's "celebration" and "assimilation" of Hispanics and their culture.

They offer platforms from which politicians can make the Salsafication-As-Measure-Of-Hispanic-Progress speech, a speech given greater urgency these days, as we have said, because of growing Hispanic political power.

The role of Hispanic Heritage Month and community *fiestas* in crowding out and closing off the inclusion of substantive Hispanic issues in the local or national agenda should not be underestimated.

For they can—in the "salsafication" speeches—be eloquently portrayed as the *expression* of a community's or country's will and pride instead of as the quite legitimate effort to have some fun with a Latin flavor.

Obviously, there is nothing wrong with wanting to enjoy oneself (as a Hispanic or non-Hispanic) at a community-wide *fiesta*. When the *meaning* of what is happening becomes applied to mercenary political purposes, however, it is time to worry. For confusing one thing with another, taking the Hispanic Resonance from one place in the popular imagination to another to deploy it (like a crack military unit) wherever else it might be needed, is a growing commonplace in the celebrated political use of a pop culture-inspired "salsafication."

There is no reason citywide or nationwide *fiestas* (as in Hispanic Heritage Month) cannot co-exist with other community activities targeted at giving voice to Hispanic concerns or at helping troubled Hispanic teenagers, say.

But with limited resources and energies, a city's choice of a *fiesta* (to which non-Hispanics will more likely "sign on" to in anticipation of the pleasant sensory sensations to be had) is much more likely to be its observance of Hispanic Heritage than seminars or community "dialogues" on Hispanic concerns.

As we have said, there has never been a time in America when non-Hispanics have such a ready reply to Hispanic doubts about whether their participation in American life is truly welcomed, locally or nationally.

Boy, do I envy you. You've got this annual event paying tribute to your spirit and culture! I wish I were Hispanic, growing up eating great food and hearing all the Latin music and learning all the Latin dances…

When this kind of fawning approval of Hispanics—as in the current "celebration" of Hispanics in the nation's ongoing "salsafication"—convinces more than a few Hispanics (as it seems to have done) it accomplishes other more strategic goals.

It substitutes, in the public policy debate, for the genuine examination of real Hispanic issues like education and employment.

Any effort to combat the "creep" of "salsafication's" *meaning* into the political arena must start with this essential point. The idea of "salsafication" as a *social movement* empowering Hispanics is a dangerous one, in part, because it *displaces* the discussion of actual Hispanic issues.

And there is a lot more to this than might be thought.

If the "assimilation" of Hispanics is a *done deal*, if "salsafication" shows it is at least proceeding apace, then there is no reason to trigger the mechanisms involved in looking at other models of Hispanic "assimilation" or "participation" in American life.

Like, say, *thinking*.

For "salsafication" as *theory*, as "assimilationist *model*"—replacing the need for any other comprehensive framework or plan for empowering Hispanics beginning with just talking about alternative strategies and scenarios—is elevated into a displacement of Hispanic ideas in the ongoing "public policy" debate at every level of our nation.

The idea of *forward movement* for Hispanics in the social and political *interpretation* of "salsafication" clearly aims to supersede, to *silence*, voices with different visions of the Hispanic (and nation's) future.

It is clearly a race, with "salsafication *theorists*" (like some politicians and Hispanic entertainers) attempting to "head off" at "the pass"—to borrow an image from "Western" movies—Hispanic activists who are working to rally Hispanic-Americans to exercise their potential for social change and political action ((before being completely captured by the happy *daydream* of progress in "salsafication").

For Hispanics (and other thoughtful Americans) who are concerned about the Hispanic future in America, there is no way to avoid the issues involved in America's ongoing "Fiesta."

For everyone else, not to worry. The "Fiesta" will find you. Party hearty.

D. Russell Martinez

ABOUT THE AUTHOR

D. Russell Martinez has written extensively on Hispanics for newspapers, magazines and U.S. Government agencies.

His work has been syndicated by the Los Angeles Times Newspaper Syndicate through its "Hispanic Link" column feature, appearing in such major newspapers as the *San Diego Union* and the *San Antonio Express-News*.

He has also written "Op-Ed" columns for the *Baltimore Sun* and *Denver Post* newspapers, worked as a "stringer" for *Newsweek* magazine, and contributed to *Americas*, the magazine of the Organization of American States. In 1984, he contributed to the book *Portraits of the Puerto Rican Experience*. His writing career began in earnest at age nineteen when he joined the Riverside, California *Press-Enterprise* newspaper as a part-time general assignment reporter while still attending Riverside City College.

As the daily newspaper's only Latino or bilingual writer, he was quickly thrust into covering (on a full-time basis) the turbulent struggle of the Chicano Civil Rights Movement and of Cesar Chavez to organize farmworkers toiling in the county's lucrative grape growing agribusiness industry.

His reporting from the front lines takes on a new dimension with this book, in which the front lines of the Hispanic Civil Rights Movement are often in our pop and political cultures.